INSANE ASYLUM

ENTERPRISE ST.

JEFFERSON ST.

AVE.

PLUM ST.

PROSPECT

ST.

CARTER ST.

PARK ST.

ADDITION ST.

NORTH ST.

DIVISION ST.

CHICAGO ST.

DU PAGE ST.

ST.

HILL ST.

WARWICK ST.

VILLA

GIFFORD ST.

PORTER

CUMBERLINE

HUNTER ST.

CHICAGO

ROAD

ROAD

RAYMOND ST.

YARWOOD ST.

ST. CHARLES

SHERMAN AVE.

LIBERTY

DEL. BY A. RUPPEL

N,

INOIS.

15211

On behalf of the Board of Directors, officers and employees of
NBD Bank Elgin, formerly The First National Bank of Elgin,
we are pleased to present to our customers and friends…

OLD ELGIN: A PICTORIAL HISTORY.

Through its pages, Elgin's rich and vibrant
history comes alive and NBD Bank Elgin is proud to have
played a vital, long-standing role in that heritage and growth.

NBD Bank Elgin hopes this
beautifully-illustrated and well-documented volume
will prove a cherished addition to your family library
and a valuable collectors' item in the years to come.

Robert H. Carlile
President and Chief Executive Officer
NBD Bank Elgin
Elgin, Illinois

NBD Bank Elgin, N.A.

FORMERLY FIRST NATIONAL BANK OF ELGIN
Established in 1865

Six Fountain Square Plaza
Elgin, IL 60120
Member FDIC

Your Neighborhood bank with world-class resources.

Old Elgin:

A Pictorial History

by
E. C. Alft

G. Bradley Publishing, Inc.
St. Louis, Missouri

Old Elgin:
A PICTORIAL HISTORY

by
E. C. Alft

A limited edition of 2,500
of which this is...

2005

Publication Staff:
Author: E. C. Alft
Cover Artist: Gary Butler
Book Design: Diane Kramer
Publisher: G. Bradley Publishing, Inc.
Sponsor: NBD Bank of Elgin

ISBN 0-943963-22-2
Printed in the United States of America

TABLE OF CONTENTS

PREFACE

Like an old family picture album, this book illustrates a by-gone Elgin. For the most part it pictures buildings that no longer exist or that have been converted from their original uses. How they once appeared would have been lost to us if professional and amateur photographers had not captured them on film and collectors had not preserved them.

Many of these pictures were taken by the cameras of five skilled men. Canadian-born John Manly Adams (1833-1901) established a photographic gallery at the north-east end of the Chicago Street bridge about 1861. By the early eighties, his son, Spencer M. Adams (1852-1922) had assumed management of the business. Arthur E. Eck (1883-1962) was a watch worker and amateur photographer who took pictures of the Elgin Road Races. The ravages of the Palm Sunday tornado were recorded by B.M. (Bert) Pease (1887-1956), a photo-engraver and professional photographer. H. Clayton Wood (1916-1988) photographed scenes of the Song of Hiawatha pageant.

Carlos H. Smith (1849-1915), a watch factory official, collected the Adams prints. After his death, his widow presented a three-volume, leather-bound edition to the Gail Borden Public Library. Elmer Gylleck (1890-1988), an architect, purchased the glass plate negatives of John and Spencer Adams, the start of a collection that eventually comprised thousands of plates and prints.

The Elgin Area Historical Society has received both the Gylleck collection and more than 100,000 negatives from the files of the *Daily Courier-News*. Clarence Reber, past president of the Society, who has been accessioning these huge acquisitions, has co-operated in selecting prints to be reproduced for this book. Cliff E. Lohs, for forty years a staff photographer for the *Courier-News*, did the photo copying. Howard Gusler allowed the use of some pictures from his extensive collection and the *Courier-News* loaned some prints from the paper's files. Mr. and Mrs. Clyde Wells and Mr. and Mrs. Stanley Hulke also made significant contributions.

Once again the author is grateful to the staff of the Gail Borden Public Library, where I have long encamped at the microfilm readers, and to the journalists who have produced the papers of record.

In the spring of 1832 Black Hawk, a Sauk Indian, his armed braves and their families, crossed the Mississippi and entered Illinois in violation of a treaty. Moving up the valley of the Rock River, they frightened the scattered white settlers. The regular Army detachments from the East that came to reinforce militiamen in the resulting war carried home descriptions of the fertile soil of Illinois.

Black Hawk's defeat opened the way to white penetration. Western farm and town sites could be purchased from the government for $1.25 per acre, and the little lake port of Chicago became the center of a land craze. A steady stream of emigrants passed through the mud and chaos of this strategically located village at the head of a proposed canal and the hub of projected railroads.

Two brothers from upstate New York, James and Hezekiah Gifford, were among those gripped by the prevailing hunger for land. They arrived at what is now the site of Elgin on April 3, 1835. James was determined to establish a town and Hezekiah a farm.

In a letter to his family back East on April 11th, James Gifford emphasized that his claim along the Fox River was on a direct line between Chicago and the lead mines of Galena, near the Mississippi. He assumed that the state legislature would establish a road between these settlements. Equally significant, his claim was "the best place for water power which I have found on the river from its source to some distance below this."

The Giffords met Joseph Kimball from New Hampshire in Chicago and invited him to join their venture on Fox River. Kimball claimed land on the west bank and was later to be joined by two sons. "James T. Gifford, Esq., from New York, near Utica, has a location on the east side of the river," he wrote one of them on July 4, 1835, "and we have agreed to build a dam together. Then, Mr. Gifford is to build a flour mill and we are to build a saw mill."

James T. Gifford, Elgin's founder, was a surveyor and skilled mechanic. Devoutly religious, he named his town after "Elgin," his favorite Scotch hymn tune. Gifford boarded newcomers and donated lots for schools and churches. He was the town's first postmaster and served as a justice of the peace. An opponent of slavery, he was an early member of the Liberty Party in Illinois.

Samuel Jewett Kimball arrived in the Fox River valley as early as 1834, driving a team from his New Hampshire home. He returned East, and then settled on Elgin's west side after the death of his father, Joseph, in 1835. A farmer and the city's second mayor, he co-operated with James T. Gifford in developing the settlement. A son, Walter, was the first white male child born in Elgin.

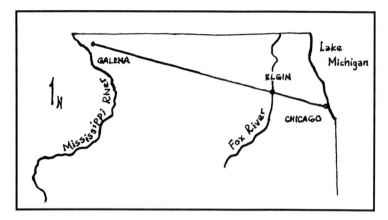

"We think that Chicago will be one of the most important places in all of the western country," wrote Joseph Kimball in the letter of July 4, 1835. "Also Galena on the Mississippi River, where the great mining country is situated, is fast increasing and will soon be a great place. We have taken considerable pains to ascertain what chance there is for making a road in direct line from Chicago to Galena and find that we are on the direct route between those two important places."

"The Fox is the finest stream I ever saw," wrote James Gifford in his letter of April 11, 1835, "it has uniformly in this State, a limestone bottom, its current uniform and gentle, its waters pure, and is abundantly supplied with fine fish. We have selected for sites to build upon, an elevation of from thirty to forty rods from it, a grove lying between."

James T. Gifford's cabin, erected after Hezekiah's, was built under an oak tree which dropped its acorns on the roof. The interior was one big room and in each corner was a bed supported by the log walls. A loft was under the roof, and the puncheon floor consisted of split logs pressed into the ground with the flat side up.

The cabin, shown here in a reconstruction for Elgin's centennial celebration in 1935, served as the town's first school, first church when the Congregationalists organized in 1836, and the first post office after the mail began arriving in 1837.

In the summer of 1836 the Elgin settlers helped mark a rough thoroughfare east to Meacham's Grove, now Bloomingdale, where a road led to Chicago. James Gifford and Sam Kimball then blazed a trail to Belvidere. This was designated a state road, the general path now followed by Highway 20. Elgin became a main crossing point on the Fox for travellers heading West.

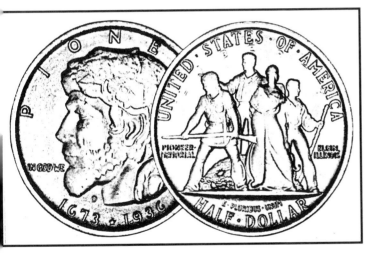

A Pioneer Memorial monument was designed by a local sculptor, Trygve Rovelstad, in the thirties. The four-figure statuary group comprised a scout or huntsman and a family of settlers. The city council designated the site without appropriating funds for its casting and base. Rovelstad modeled a commemorative half dollar depicting the monument to mark Elgin's centennial in 1935. Congress, however, didn't pass the enabling legislation until 1936. The Philadelphia mint produced 25,000, plus fifteen for assay purposes. Purchased from the mint for fifty cents, the coins were to be sold for $1.50. This was a considerable sum during the Depression, and 5,000 unsold coins had to be sent back to the mint for re-melting. Because of the small number circulated, the value of the Elgin Commemorative Half Dollar has risen over the years.

Numismatists occasionally pass through town and inquire about the monument on the coin, but it was never cast. His life-long dream unfulfilled, Rovelstad–pictured here with his daughter, Gloria,—died in 1990. The huge twelve-foot figures remain in his studio. Rovelstad was also a medalist, the designer of the Second World War infantryman's combat badge.

William C. Kimball, an older brother of Sam, arrived in 1837, opened a store, and entered claims for huge tracts on the west side. In 1845 he erected the Waverly flour mills (above) along the west side race, north of what is now Highland Avenue.

The settlement's first bridge, a crude wooden affair that had to stretch over a river much wider than it is now, was built at Chicago Street in 1837-38. It went out in the 1849 flood and had to be replaced by this span. Pedestrians were protected from teams and cattle by a formidable barrier. The eastern end reached almost to Market Square. On the hill to the left can be seen the first railroad depot.

The dam raised the river's surface to a higher level and allowed the water to fall into narrow raceways constructed on both sides of the river. The water rushing through these races powered the mill wheels. This is the east side race as it appeared in 1952. The site was about 100 feet north of Highland Avenue and just west of North Grove Avenue. The race, now filled, once extended from the dam to the south side of East Chicago Street.

The woolen mill, Elgin's first major industry, was constructed over the east side mill race north of the bridge in 1843-44. It was enlarged and a tower and clock added in 1866-67.

The building was purchased by the David C. Cook Publishing Co. in 1882 and remained part of their plant until 1901, when it was bought by the YMCA. The Y used the premises until 1956. The old landmark was razed in 1965 for the extension of Riverside Drive.

Captured by Rodolphus W. Padelford (left), Elgin's first "daguerrean artist," in 1847 is a view of the town looking east across the Fox. In the left foreground is William C. Kimball's store and one corner of his Waverly Mill, both on the west side of the river. Visible to the right is the long wooden bridge. Along what is now South Grove Avenue are farm implement shops. In the upper center, at Chicago and Spring streets, is B.W. Raymond's store. At the far left is the woolen factory. Its dry-house, on the river's edge, is not yet under roof.

Old Brick, an early school building, was completed in 1847 and opened January 3, 1848. It stood on the northeast corner of DuPage and Chapel streets and was torn down in 1884. Old Brick was at first supported by private subscription; public-supported education in Elgin did not begin until 1851.

The New Brick school was opened in 1857 on Kimball Street near Center. The frame section on the north side was added in 1873. The building was razed about 1899 to provide the site for the Abby Wing school.

Benjamin W. Raymond never lived in Elgin, but his monied connections helped transform a rural settlement into an industrial city. A mayor of Chicago, he bought part of James Gifford's claim and opened a store in Elgin in 1839. He was instrumental in establishing a local foundry and tannery as well as the woolen mill. A director of the Galena & Chicago Union, the first railroad to be constructed west of Chicago, he was influential in routing the line through Elgin. It was, after all, the direction Gifford had foreseen in laying out his town. Raymond was president of the Fox River Valley Railroad which built a line from Elgin north to the Wisconsin border beginning in 1854. Both roads were later merged with the Chicago & North Western.

The arrival of the Galena & Chicago Union, which reached Elgin in 1850, ensured the permanence of the settlement and sparked a building boom. The railroad's first locomotive, the *Pioneer*, was a wood burner with six wheels, two of them drivers. It weighed about ten tons and had a top speed of twenty-five miles per hour. The *Pioneer*, which had been built for another railroad in 1836, was retired from service in 1873 and is on display at the Chicago Historical Society.

By the time the G&CU arrived in Elgin, the railroad had two eight wheelers, the *Chicago* and the *Elgin*, in addition to the *Pioneer*. According to an 1851 time table, the run to Chicago took three hours; by 1856, however, scheduled time on a fast express had been reduced to two hours and nine minutes.

With the coming of the railroad, William C. Kimball built the four-story brick Waverly in 1852-53 on the southwest corner of Broadway (now North State Street) and Galena (now West Highland Avenue). A veranda (shown left) overlooked an ample lawn, shaded with trees, to the south. The Waverly had a large dining room, a ballroom that could accommodate 100 dancers, and a rather steep daily rate of $2.

The Waverly's fire-resistant cobblestone stable, still standing, can be seen in this view from the north. Steps in the rear led to the "high" North Western tracks. Early day trains allowed passengers to stop for refreshments. Chicagoans were attracted by the Waverly's pure spring water and the fresh country air, and local residents considered it an ideal place for banquets and dances.

The hotel was purchased by the city for use as a court and lockup in 1884. When Salvation Army members were arrested for disturbing the peace on Fountain Square, one of those jailed at the Waverly was young Eddie Parker, a local printer's devil. One day he would become the Army's national commander.

The Waverly subsequently became a factory producing condensed milk and malted milk. It was razed in 1917.

William S. Shaw erected the Elgin House on the northeast corner of Center and East Chicago Streets about 1840. In 1852 it was purchased and remodeled for the Elgin Seminary for young ladies established by Emily and Ellen Ford the previous year. The school was continued until the summer of 1856, when the Elgin Academy was under construction. Myra Colby Bradwell, a student and afterward a teacher at the Seminary, passed the bar examination in 1869 but was denied admission by the Illinois Supreme Court on the ground that she was a woman.

The building again became a hotel and boarding house. The above picture was taken in the seventies. At the right is the First Baptist Church, dedicated in 1871. The old hotel was razed for the construction of the First Congregational Church, which now occupies the site.

About 1844 William S. Shaw built a hotel on a Chicago Street lot that was to become the right of way for the "low" (east side) North Western. This was rebuilt just to the east of the tracks and became known as the City Hotel. It was one of the three voting places in the first city election in 1854. Family tradition held that Ulysses Grant was once a guest when he was a salesman and hide buyer for his brother's Galena leather store.

At Shaw's hotel, boarders unable to pay their rent promptly were moved to the top floor until they paid in full. This was to save the cash customers the trouble of climbing stairs and also made it more difficult to get the patron's baggage out if he decided to skip.

Shaw's, later known as the Commercial, was razed in 1902.

The Kimball House opened in 1855 on the northeast corner of Douglas Avenue and North Street. Like many other local hotels, it was renamed by successive proprietors. Known later as the Burns, Ramsay, New Douglas, and the Northway, it was razed in 1966. The Kimball sheltered some of the former slaves, called contrabands during the Civil War, the night of their arrival in Elgin in 1862 and thereby acquired the erroneous reputation of being a station on the Underground Railroad.

OLD MAIN

Elgin was a raw western settlement when its Academy was chartered by the state legislature in 1839. Instruction did not begin until Old Main opened its doors in December 1856. The entrance columns and the gabled roof place it in the Greek Revival style popular in the middle years of the last century.

This was one of the first private schools open to students of all religious faiths. In the early days Old Main housed the entire Academy. The east wing of the first floor was occupied by the principal and his family. The west wing was used as a student dormitory, and classes were held upstairs. Students pored over their books at night by candles or fluid lamps.

Lightning struck the bell tower of Old Main on the night of August 17, 1911. Before the fire fighters could arrive, delayed by the storm that put two of the fire alarm circuits out of commission, the entire roof and third floor were in flames. The old bell fell into the ground floor, its casting broken. Damage done by water equalled the destruction by fire.

The reconstruction substituted a flat roof for the gabled roof, thereby erasing the integrity of the Greek Revival appearance. In 1969 Old Main was closed and slated for demolition. It was instead deeded to the city of Elgin, and, in 1976-77, funds were raised for its restoration as the community's American Revolution Bicentennial project.

The exterior of Old Main was restored in 1979-80. Although the original chimneys were not replaced, the gabled roof was reproduced and a new plastic cupola lifted into place. Paint was removed to reveal the original brick, and new windows were installed. The first floor was finished in 1987 and occupied by the Elgin Area Historical Society. The second floor was completed in 1991. Flood-lighted at night, the building is once again a landmark on Elgin's east side.

Lawrence, Molony & Co's distillery occupied about 500 feet of the west side riverfront just above the dam. The plant could process up to 1,000 bushels of grain daily and made its own barrels. Cattle were fed on the refuse. When the Lincoln administration enacted a wartime tax on distilled spirits, some time elapsed between the passage of the levy and its effective date. During the interval, Benjamin Lawrence and Walter Pease, the two local proprietors, filled cellars and barns with kegs of their product. The day after the new rates were imposed, they began selling their immense stock at an advance of two dollars per gallon over the previous price. By the time their inventory was sold, they were wealthy men. Their earnings were used to purchase stock in the new watch factory and to establish the First National Bank. The distillery was destroyed by fire in 1870.

A frame building surmounted by a small tower was raised in 1838, chiefly through the liberality of James Gifford. Called the Union Chapel because it was occupied jointly by the Congregationalists and Baptists, the first two churches to be formed, it was used as a schoolhouse during the week days.

Pictured above is the first building used exclusively for church purposes. It was erected by the Methodists on a lot donated by James Gifford. It was known as the Buttermilk Church because it was painted white with whitewash and buttermilk.

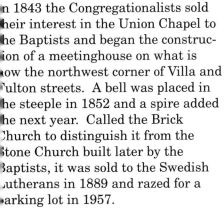

n 1843 the Congregationalists sold heir interest in the Union Chapel to he Baptists and began the construc- ion of a meetinghouse on what is now the northwest corner of Villa and Fulton streets. A bell was placed in he steeple in 1852 and a spire added he next year. Called the Brick Church to distinguish it from the Stone Church built later by the Baptists, it was sold to the Swedish Lutherans in 1889 and razed for a parking lot in 1957.

The Baptists erected a cobblestone hurch on Geneva Street in 1849. After they moved to a new building n East Chicago Street in 1870, the Old Stone Church—its steeple removed and a second floor insert- d—became a public school. It was orn down in 1892 after Franklin chool was occupied.

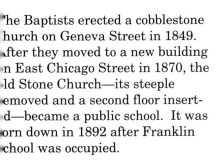

Many of the scenes of early Elgin were recorded by John Manly Adams and his son, Spencer M. Adams. The father arrived in Elgin with his parents in 1843. He successively pursued the trades of mattress maker, plasterer and butcher until he learned the art of photography about 1861.

Spencer (Pent) Adams, the son, had become the firm's chief photographer by the early eighties. One of the younger Adams' last assignments was providing more than 125 photographs of Elgin scenes for a chamber of commerce type publication in 1914.

The J. M. Adams "Photographic Art Gallery" was opened at the east end of the Chicago Street bridge in 1864. At the roof's north end was the skylight. An enlarger is on display behind the team and wagon. Adams specialized in *cartes de visite* and ambrotypes. Later he moved to a building on the south side of the street.

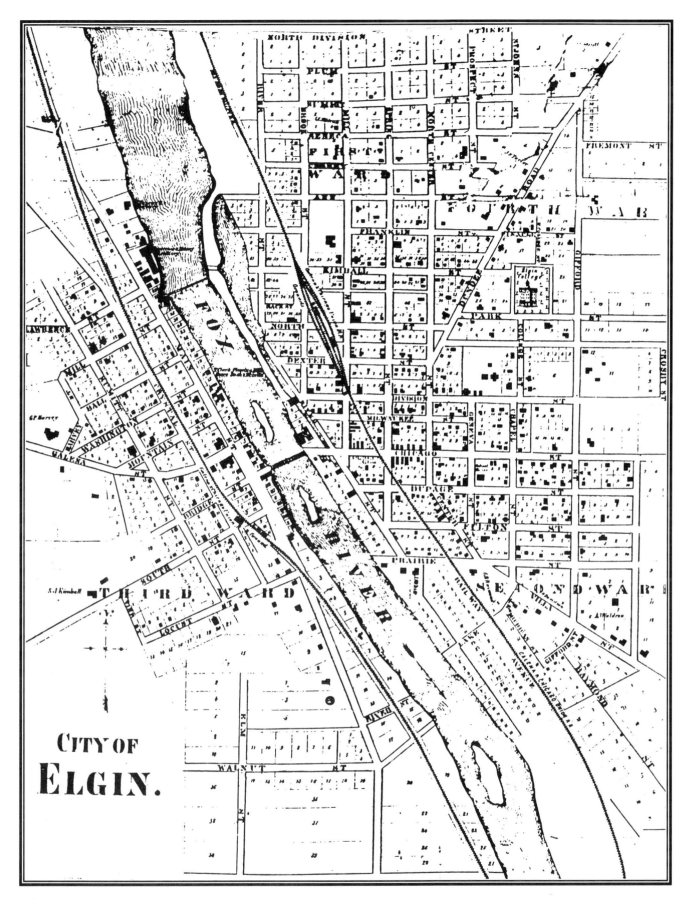

CITY OF ELGIN.

The federal census reported, somewhat inaccurately, that ,797 persons were living in Elgin in 1860. More than a ourth were foreign born, chiefly Irish, German and British. The city's economy was based on processing and transport-ng the surplus production "grains, milk and wool" of sur-ounding farms. Grain not turned into flour at the four iver mills was converted into alcohol at the distillery, and the wool was made into flannel. Already milk was being shipped daily into Chicago. The farmer's needs were also supplied by agricultural machinery and wagon shops. Most residents lived within half a mile of Market Square, and about three fourths of the dwellings were located on the east side. The community was served by two railroads, a weekly newspaper, four schoolhouses, an Academy, and six churches.

Civil War

The Civil War was a great dividing line in the history of Elgin, transforming a rural mill town into an industrial city. An inflow of money from high wheat and milk prices, combined with the windfall profits of the distillery, provided the local capital to attract manufacturers. Before the end came at Appomatto, watch-makers were arriving from the East to equip big factory on the old Dexter farm to the south of town

To commemorate the Elgin lives lost in the conflict, two 30-pound Parrott guns were obtained from the Rock Island arsenal in 1897. Used during the war, they were placed in the Soldiers Reserve at Bluff City Cemetery.

Elgin troops fought in the West, where the war was won. Co. K, 52nd Illinois Volunteer Infantry, is shown here lined up at Market Square. Its captai John S. Wilcox, advanced t the rank of colonel. Major losses were incurred at Shiloh, Corinth and the Atlanta campaign. The reg iment marched with Sherman to Savannah and the sea. (Courtesy Illinois State Historical Society)

Col. William F. Lynch left his studies at Notre Dame to command the 58th Illinois. The unit was captured at Shiloh after sustaining heavy losses. Other Elgin enlistments served in the battle-hardened 36th and 127th Illinois.

The 141st Illinois was mustered in for a hundred days' service in 1864 and was assigned to guard duty in occupied territory. Elgin enlistments were in Companies A, C and G.

Portraits are the main source of income for most professional photographers, but the Adams' cameras (see page 20) were also focused upon the changing cityscape of Elgin. A panorama in 1866 encompassed the east side from the far north end to the newly-erected watch factory along what is now National Street.

From left to right in the first section are west side stores, the dam and mill pond (to be called the Dipper), and the Chicago Street bridge. At the east end of the bridge are the two woolen factory buildings, the Adams gallery, and the City Mills. The latter, like the woolen mill, built over the east side mill race and was the largest of the four grist mills. It had a daily capacity of 100 barrels. At the right, along the river bank, is a temporary wooden building where the first tools and machinery were made for the watch factory. At the edge of the picture is Orlando Davidson's bank building at the north end of Market square, the city's geographic center.

The two steeples belong to the Stone Church (Baptist), on the left at Geneva Street near DuPage, and to the Brick Church (Congregational) at Villa and Fulton.

This section of the panorama begins at Market Square and clearly show Hubbard's building, occupied by Newman and Innes, on the northeast corner. Across the street, on the southeast corner, was Sherman Hall, a three-story wooden building. Access to the second floor was gained by an outside stairway. Visible at left center is Shaw's hotel at the southwest corner of Spring and Chicago, and diagonally across the street is the two-story store building erected by B. W. Raymond. On its hilltop, center right, is the Academy. The large two-story Elgin House, below and to the right, is at the northeast corner of Center and Chicago.

The west side was less settled than the east side, although it was the location of the "high" North Western train station, Kimball's mill, and the distillery.

COBBLESTONES

Cobblestone homes arose in western New York following completion of the Erie Canal in 1825. Unemployed masons, who had been recruited to build the locks and bridge abutments, purchased farms in the area and built homes of small fieldstones to supplement their incomes. Rounded and uncut, they provided a facing for a kind of cement or rubblestone wall. About ninety percent of all cobblestone structures are located within a radius of about sixty miles centered on Rochester.

Elgin had more residents from New York in 1840 and 1850 than from any other state. Some of these Yorkers brought with them a preference for cobblestone construction they had known back East. Fieldstones, turned up by the plow or found along the river banks, were abundant in the vicinity, and there were New York-trained masons in the settlement.

Cobblestone masonry has "V"-shaped horizontal and vertical joints which make the cobblestones project slightly from the wall. Each stone has a highlighted and shaded area which change with the direction of the sun.

Cobblestone buildings, like those made of brick, were fireproof and required no painting, but they were much less costly. The stones, which did not have to be shaped and kiln dried, were sorted into uniform sizes with the use of boards containing holes with different circumferences. The walls were usually a foot to sixteen inches thick. Cut limestone from quarries was used at the corners, where the cobblestones could have been easily dislodged, and for lintels above the window and door openings.

Advertisement appearing in the *Elgin Gazette,* February 4, 1857.

"The Stone Cottage" was erected for James T. Gifford, Elgin's founder, in 1849-50. Its original design was inspired by the architecture he had admired during a sojourn in South Carolina as a young man. His son-in-law, Orlando Davidson, later added a new wing and mansard roof to the combination of Southern columns and New York-style cobblestone. After Davidson's death in 1899, the Stone Cottage with its grounds, carriage house, and servant quarters were sold to developers who parceled the area into building lots and divided the house into apartments. The home is still standing at 363-365 Prairie Street. It was placed on the National Register of Historic Places in 1980.

Elgin's first mayor, Dr. Joseph Tefft, emigrated from Madison County, New York. Between 1846 and 1849 he erected a cobblestone and brick home on what is now East Highland Avenue. It was purchased by the First Methodist Church in 1914 and used as a parish house until it was razed in 1923 preparatory to the erection of the present church building.

The home of Reuben Yardwood, who was manager of the woolen mill, was located at the intersection of Division Street and the North Western right of way. It was razed to clear a site for the Fox Hotel in 1924. Of the more than twenty cobblestone structures erected in Elgin, only six homes and the facade of a livery stable survive.

One of the oldest Elgin homes was a cobblestone on the northwest corner of West Chicago and North Crystal streets. It was erected about 1846-48 by Samuel J. and William C. Kimball for their mother, Nancy Currier Kimball. Converted to a rooming house, it was extensively damaged by fire caused by careless use of smoking materials on August 15, 1991.

A cousin of Samuel J. and William C. Kimball, Edson A. Kimball lived in this cobblestone at what is now 328 Mountain Street. He ran a hardware store for many years and was a member of the first City Council in 1854.

MILK & BUTTER

2

Elgin's development as a dairying center began in 1852 with the first shipment of milk by train to the fast growing city of Chicago. When supplies of fluid milk began to exceed demand, two new markets opened up for the farmer. Gail Borden, the inventor of a process for condensing milk, established a plant in Elgin in 1865. As industrialization crowded families into cities, few had access to fresh milk or the means of keeping it safe to use. Borden's "canned milk," pure and uniform in quality, was especially nutritious for children.

Another outlet was provided by the little butter and cheese factories which sprang up in northern Illinois. Although one was located in Elgin, most of them operated in rural areas for close access to the milk supply. The output of these creameries was sold on the Elgin Board of Trade, formed in 1872 as a meeting place for buyers and sellers. Prices set on this exchange soon governed the butter markets of the country, especially in the West and South. In 1890 more than 24 million pounds of butter and 5 million pounds of cheese were sold on the Board.

Twenty-five years after the first milk was sent to Chicago, there were at least 12,000 cows in Elgin Township. Increased attention was given to the improvement of dairy herds. In 1874 the first Holsteins arrived in the area for breeding purposes, and several stock farms became major suppliers of dairy cows.

Within the city of Elgin other industries served the farmers and creamery operators. Two big factories turned out butter tubs and cheese boxes, and several shops produced milk cans, strainers, vats, coolers, steam engines to power churns, and other equipment. The *Elgin Dairy Report* ("Elgin Makes the Price, We Tell You What It Is"), widely circulated, published news about the industry.

Elgin Pattern.

Progress over forty years is evident in the drawing at the left of the first can of milk sent to Chicago by train on February 12, 1852 and the 1892 can, invented and patented by Frank Shepherd of Elgin, at the right.

Early in the morning, when it was still cool, farmers would load milk cans in wagons to trundle them over country roads to a rail head, a creamery, or a condenser. The Borden operation in Elgin alone received milk from more than a hundred dairy farms.

Dr. Joseph Tefft emigrated to Illinois by ox team with his father's family in 1835. He first located in South Elgin but removed to Elgin in 1838 and erected the first frame house. Tefft's medical practice extended over a wide area. His journeys were made on an old gray horse, which was well known by the early settlers.

In 1854 he was elected the first mayor of the newly incorporated city of Elgin. Tefft was the first president of the Elgin Board of Trade and served nine years guiding the exchange toward national recognition. The owner of a dairy farm, Tefft was elected president of the Illinois Holstein Breeders Association when it was formed in Elgin in 1885.

Joseph Tefft's interests weren't confined to medicine, politics and the dairy industry. In 1855 he became president of the board of trustees of Elgin Academy and held that position for thirty-three years. He was the first president of the Elgin Packing Company and for many years headed the Old Settlers' Association.

The first steam-operated butter factory west of the Great Lakes was opened in 1870 at Harvey and Ball streets by the Elgin Dairy Co. The product was far superior to hand-churned butter. In 1874 the plant's capacity was 2,000 gallons of milk daily, and six to eight hands turned out 144,000 pounds of butter and 190,000 pounds of cheese. Refuse from this creamery flowed into Buttermilk Creek and may have given the vicinity its Slop Hill designation.

This imposing three-story and basement building was erected in 1892-93 by the Elgin Butter Co., which controlled the output of about fifty creameries. Its huge separator could skim five tons of milk per hour, and its churns had a capacity of about half a ton per churning. Because of the weight, the butter making equipment was located in the basement, while the upper floors were used for storage. In its final days, before it was razed in 1965 for the Civic Center, it had been converted to a tenement.

Delmont E. Wood and William W. Sherwin, creamery operators, formed a partnership and in 1881-82 erected a cold storage warehouse at Lawrence Avenue and North State Street. The third floor housed 2,000 tons of ice, and the lower floors had a 100-car load capacity. They also engaged in the manufacture of butter tubs and cheese boxes. Their plant, below, was sold to the Creamery Package Manufacturing Co. of Chicago, which Wood and Sherwin helped to organize, but it continued operating locally until 1926. About 1890 it was employing seventy and turning out 500,000 tubs and 10,000 boxes annually.

The Elgin Butter Tub Co. was an outgrowth of a strike by coopers at the Wood & Sherwin plant. At its peak of production in the mid-twenties, annual output approximated 2,000,000 tubs. They were made in 10, 20, 30, 40 and 63-pound sizes, about ninety percent in the largest size. No nails were used in their construction, although brads were used in sewing the rim around the cover. The accurately planed and jointed staves were compressed together, either steel or wood hoops holding the container in rigid form.

Sylvester S. Mann, who served three terms in the state legislature, was a creamery operator and cattle breeder. In 1883 he went to Europe and purchased 160 Holsteins, importing them directly to Elgin from Holland. He erected a huge, 100 feet by 40 feet two-story barn in back of his home on Division Street. (This was before zoning laws were enacted.) The barn was destroyed by fire in 1890. This picture was taken in 1884 from an electric arc light tower.

JOHN NEWMAN

Born in England, John Newman arrived in Elgin in 1864 to invest his savings in a dry goods store. Although he continued to operate this business until 1898, as his means increased he began buying or leasing creameries. His first purchase was the Spring Brook factory in 1876.

By 1898 the John Newman Co., with offices overlooking Fountain Square, owned or controlled fifty-two creameries scattered over northern Illinois, eastern Iowa, and southern Wisconsin. Some 55,000 cows pastured on more that 2,000 farms provided half a million quarts of milk daily to be made into Spring Brook brand butter. Newman served as president of the Elgin Board of Trade for seventeen years, 1894 to 1911.

A widower, John Newman in 1887 married Mrs. Laura Borden, who had divorced a son of Gail Borden. Soon after their return from a wedding trip to Europe, they began making plans for one of Elgin's finest homes. Completed in 1889-90 at 321 Division Street, the mansion had fourteen rooms and eight fireplaces. Queen Anne style features include the mixture of white brick and brownstone, high roof, polygonal turret, the onion dome, a jerkin head roof on the front dormer and full scale spindled veranda. The interior was finished in white and red oak, birch, sycamore, cypress, cherry, and Georgia pine. The stables in the rear housed some of the fine trotting horses Newman bred on his farm east of the city. The building was heavily vandalized in 1973. Restored, it opened as "The Butterman's" restaurant in 1976.

GAIL BORDEN

ail Borden spent seven years trying to shrink and preserve milk in
a airtight can, and in 1856 he succeeded by boiling out most of the
ater and adding sugar. The residue had twice the strength and
chness of cream. Increased demand during the Civil War taxed the
pacity of his plants in Connecticut and New York. Learning about
e dairy farms in the Fox valley from his third wife, who had lived in
lgin, he opened a factory in a converted Elgin tannery in 1865.

orden was strict about the cleanliness of the supplying farms and
e health of their cows. His inspectors demanded sterilized milk
ns and immaculate barns. He often visited Elgin on business, but
e heart of his empire remained in New York, and he spent his win-
rs in Texas.

he Illinois Condensed Milk Co., the
orporate name of the local Borden
ndenser, in 1889 consumed 40,000
uarts of milk daily to produce 700
ses of 48 one-pound cans. In a pro-
otion stunt in 1893 the company
aded up a train headed for San
rancisco with 55,000 cases and
dvertised it as the "largest shipment
f condensed milk from Elgin, the
reatest milk producing region on
arth."

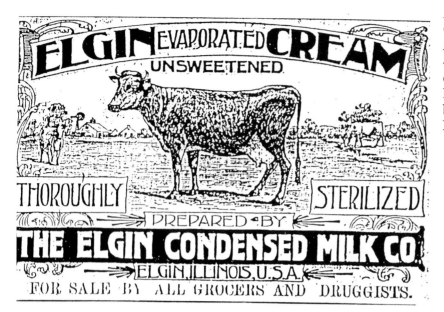

A competitor of the Borden firm, the Elgin Condensed Milk Co., began production in 1888. At its peak in the spring of 1893, it was shipping 480,000 cans of preserved milk and 144,000 cans of evaporated cream each month. In addition a large quantity of condensed milk was sent in bulk to Chicago daily. In 1894 it was sold to Borden's Illinois Condensed Milk Co.

Elgin's leadership in the Midwest dairy industry reached a peak in the nineties, when there were nearly two hundred butter and cheese factories within a radius of fifty miles around the city. After the turn of the century, the increased flow of fluid milk into the growing city of Chicago raised prices and led to a shift in butter production from the Fox valley to Wisconsin. The Board of Trade by 1910 had ceased to have any real influence over prices, and the Borden condenser closed in 1918.

The B. S. Pearsall Butter Co., a successor to Delmont Wood's operation, began making margarine in 1915. By 1926, the approximate date of the above picture, the firm was occupying 60,000 square feet of floor space in a reinforced concrete plant and was a major producer of the "substitute." Margarine is still manufactured in the same location.

ELGIN WATCHES

3

n this temporary frame building, erected early in 1865 along
he east bank of the river, the National Watch Co. began con-
tructing the tools to make its fine jeweled movements.
Three stories in height, it was structurally weak and shook
when the machinery was started. Supporting beams on
either side were necessary to brace it. When fire destroyed
art of the business district, men and women formed a bucket
rigade to save the building and its contents.

WATCHES BY THE MILLION...

For more than a century Elgin was
the home of the Elgin National Watch
Co. This enterprise transformed a
rural market town into an industrial
city, spread its name throughout the
land, and profoundly influenced the
way its people lived. Beginning in
1867, when the first watch was assem-
bled, more than fifty million jeweled
movements were produced in what
evolved into the world's largest watch
manufacturing complex.

The prosperity enjoyed by the
American Watch Co. at Waltham,
Massachusetts, during the Civil War
encouraged Chicago capitalists to
establish a competing concern in the
West. A National Watch Co. was organized in 1864. The president, Benjamin
W. Raymond, had been an early
investor in Elgin ventures and was
influential in selecting the Fox Valley
town as the site of its factory. Citizens
donated thirty-five acres of land and
subscribed to $25,000 worth of the com-
pany's stock.

Seven craftsmen were induced to
leave Waltham by a generous bonus,
increased salaries, and half-acre plots
for homes. They arrived in the winter
of 1864-65 and began making the
machines to produce the watches. In
Elgin, as at Waltham, a machine would
take the place of a tool or fixture guided
by the hand of a workman, cams and
levers replacing the eye and hand of the
operative. The result was greater accuracy in the finished time piece.

While craftsmen were building the machinery, work was started on a permanent factory facing National Street. This three-story and basement plant opened in 1866 with a two-story and basement west wing, and a two-story and basement south wing. The central portion housed the administrative offices.

In 1868 a two-story and basement east wing was added, completing the factory as it was originally designed. The stand near the fence was occupied by a band that serenaded workers at the Saturday evening closing. The railroad tracks are those of the east side, or "low," Chicago & North Western.

The first Elgin movement began ticking ten months after the new factory was occupied. Named the "B. W. Raymond" after the company's president, it was an 18-size, full plate, with quick train and straight line escapement. This 15-jewel, key-wind, key-set movement later became a popular railroad watch.

Elgin watches were originally sold uncased. The buyer selected a case at the retail store, and the jeweler cased the movement. The switch to the smaller wrist watch movements in the twenties led the factory to begin casing for greater accuracy.

The 1873-74 expansion was a practical duplicate of the original factory except that the new administrative building was larger and had a bell tower. It was connected with the first building by a wing of the same height and width as the others. The plant now formed a letter "H." It was the custom of the day to refer to a company's products by the city of manufacture. Recognizing that customers were asking for Elgins, in 1874 the firm changed its name formally to the Elgin National Watch Co.

new boiler and engine house was part of ... expansion. In 1874 a chimney stack 44 feet high was raised. It is seen at the ... ght in the process of construction. Once ... major community landmark, it was torn ... wn in 1949.

This engraving of Elgin watch workers was used to illustrate an article entitled, "Making Watches By Machinery," published in *Harper's New Monthly Magazine* in July 1869. An expert watchmaker, working by hand, might make a watch in three weeks. The Elgin factory was then turning out one movement every three and a half days for every worker in the establishment, including clerks. Eventually the output would exceed one movement per employee per day.

Early watches were thick, heavy "turnips," large in diameter, and were wound with keys. The first stem-winders were introduced in 1873. Open faced watches, such as the key-wind pictured above, became popular in the eighties. By the turn of the century, the fashion turned to watches that were thinner and smaller in diameter. Bracelet or "strap" watches for women were placed on the market in 1910. Men turned to the wrist watch during and after the First World War, and it soon displaced the pocket models.

The first Elgin-made movement, the B. W. Raymond No. 101 completed April 1, 1867, is shown at the lower right. The first lady's, also key wound, No. 40001, was completed May 20, 1869, and is shown at the upper left. Two modern watches provide a contrast.

The company's trademark featured a winged Father Time. He is holding the traditional scythe in his right hand, but an Elgin watch in his left hand has replaced the hour glass. It first appeared on the cover of an advertising almanac in 1871.

A view from the west side of the river in the eighties shows the expanded National House on the left. Goff's Island divides the National Street bridge into two sections. It was purchased by the Elgin National Watch Co. in 1888. After the turn of the century the channel between its shore line and the east bank was filled in.

In the spring of 1880 the 1100 employees were turning out 500 watches per working day. By the end of 1889, the factory's payroll had climbed to 2700, and daily output was 1650. Elgin was now the leading domestic producer of fine jeweled movements.

The next three additions were begun in 1881 and finished in 1883. The front wing was brought westward toward the river, adding a small tower, and two other wings were buil[t] on the south and east sides. The lit-tle Chicago & North Western station in the foreground was erected in 188[ ] for the convenience of employees.

At first glance the picture below is similar to the picture on page 40. But note that a third story has been added to the connecting wing in the center of the complex. This completed "the old factory" and brought the total floor space for manufacturing purposes to 175,000 square feet. The two photographs were probably taken from the roof of the National House, a company owned and operated employee boardinghouse.

George Hunter, one of the seven craftsmen who were lured from Waltham, was a machinist who became factory superintendent in 1872. When he retired in 1903, he was succeeded by his son, George E. Hunter, who retired in 1925.

Watch factory work was clean, quiet and sedentary. The ties and white shirts of these inspectors in 1892 were not unusual.

While working conditions were neat and tidy, the long, ten-hour day was not relaxed until 1899, when Saturday half holidays were allowed during the summer months. Extra pay for overtime and holidays was introduced in the spring of 1900. Employees were given the nine-hour day, with ten hours' pay, in 1901, and the eight-hour day arrived in 1917. During the prosperous twenties, the plant operated on a 5-1/2 day week.

In 1893, when this picture was taken, many of the women went to work with two petticoats, a long sweeping dress that brushed the floor, and high button shoes. Because smoking was forbidden, the men chewed tobacco. The women preferred gum.

Horse-drawn buses are awaiting fares at the National Street entrance to the watch factory. At the right is one of Bruce Payne's horsecars, which began running on South Grove Avenue between the factory and Fountain Square in 1878. The power source was unpredictable. When the brakes balked, the car banged against a horse's legs. If this occurred too often, the horse would retaliate by kicking against the dashboard.

The large building in the background behind the horsecar was the Oriental roller rink.

In 1890 the horse-drawn streetcars were replaced by the Elgin City Railway Co., an electric line. Because the cars didn't cross the National Street bridge, watch workers who lived on the west side either had to walk up the hill to Walnut and South State or take a car south to Fountain Square and transfer.

By 1930 employees were driving cars to work in large numbers.

NATIONAL HOUSE

After the National Watch Co. opened its first building, the arrival of dozens of new employees strained the little city's housing capacity. The management appropriated $10,000 for the erection of a boardinghouse across the street from the factory, between the North Western tracks and what is now Raymond Street.

The National House was operated by the company at cost, the moderate rates deducted from the employees' wages. At one time separate private rooms equipped with bathrooms and dumb-waiters were reserved for members of the board of directors when visiting the factory.

Beginning in 1919 the National House provided lodging for single women only, and in 1922 the dining room was converted into a cafeteria. Its work force drastically reduced by the Depression, the company closed the National House in 1932, and it was demolished the same year. The gymnasium was torn down in 1937, and the site was later made into an employee parking lot.

Completed in 1867, the National House was a brick building, 110 feet by 40 feet in dimension, and four stories high. It had a mansard roof with dormer windows and a piazza to the west. Many married couples, as well as single men and women, made their first home in Elgin at the National House.

44

In 1882-83, in order to keep pace with the expanding work force, a west wing, 112 feet by 30 feet, was built along the Chicago & North Western right of way. Another building, with the same dimensions but only two stories high, provided space for a new laundry and servants' quarters. The National House now had 150 lodging rooms and a dining hall with a capacity of 500.

TENNIS COURT
LADIES NATIONAL ATHLETIC CLUB
ELGIN NATIONAL WATCH Co.

A gymnasium was constructed at the east end in 1889-90. When tennis became popular, courts were constructed at the rear of the National House.

45

The National Gymnasium was connected by corridor to the National House. It was a four-story, 50 by 100 feet building. After the National House was razed in 1932, it stood alone until it, too, was torn down in 1937. The first floor was fitted up for the Elgin Watch Factory Military Band. It contained the director's office and study, a music room, a baggage room, uniform lockers, lavatories, and practice room. A ballroom, widely used for employee socials and entertainments, was on the second floor.

The third and fourth floors were equipped with machines for developing the body: a wrestling machine; a back and loin machine; traveling parallel bars; and rowing, paddling and bicycle exercise apparatus.

At the height of occupancy about the turn of the century, the dining room was staffed with 51 waiters and waitresses and could provide 1500 meals daily. To insure good quality, generous samples were delivered to the homes of company officials who lived south of the hostelry on Watch Street.

About 18,000 quarts of fruit were canned each season to be used later as preserves or in pies. Holiday meals were gastronomic events at the National House. Guests of residents were welcomed. Among the items on the Christmas menu for 1890 were mock turtle soup, baked Lake Erie trout, saute of rabbit, baked game pie, and English plum pudding.

LIBRARY
NATIONAL HOUSE.
ELGIN NATIONAL
WATCH CO.

"The rooms in the National hotel are all furnished with steam heat and modern conveniences, supplied with first-class ventilation, and there are accommodations for 350 persons," reported a Chicago newspaper in 1895. "Spacious corridors, large parlors, a well stocked library free to employees, a well equipped billiard room, office, a complete laundry, etc. are features of the hotel."

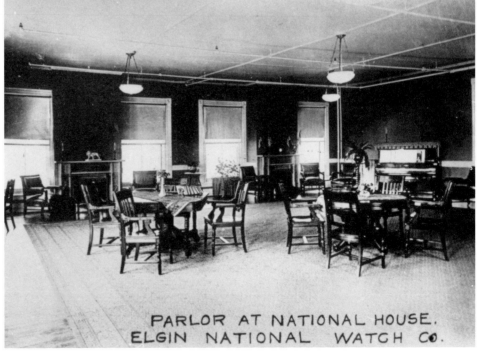

PARLOR AT NATIONAL HOUSE.
ELGIN NATIONAL WATCH CO.

William A. Gabriel, hired by the Elgin National Watch Co. in 1887 as a draftsman became the firm's famed designer before he retired in 1933.

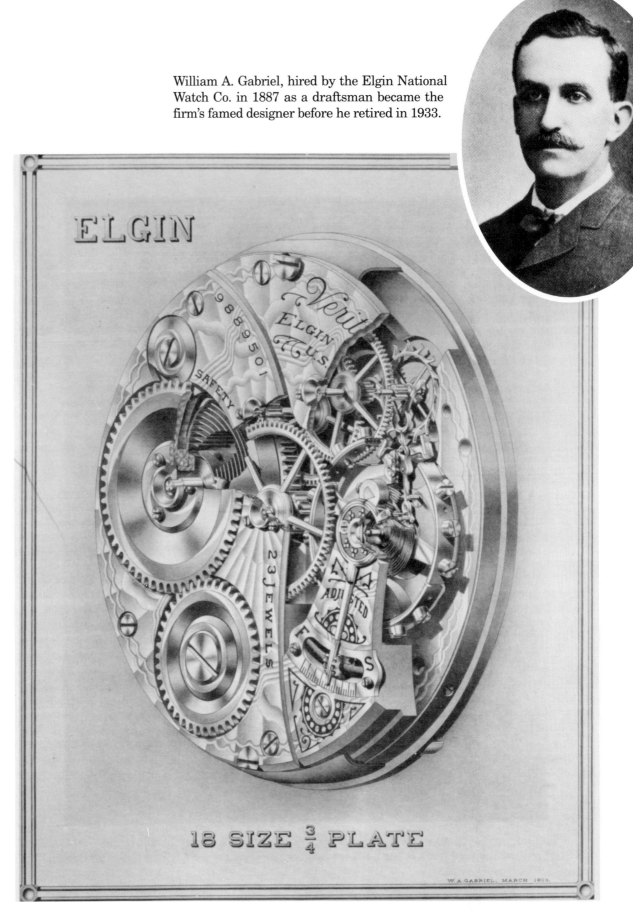

This large scale drawing of an eighteen size three-fourths plate Elgin watch was the work of its designer, William A. Gabriel. The watch appears as though turned to an angle of thirty degrees from the observer. To obtain this projection, an especially constructed ellipsograph was designed and built. Drawings of more than forty details were made from blueprints. Gabriel worked part time for more than two years on the project.

Because the construction of the old factory was highly flammable,
the company broke ground in 1902 for a modern, fire resistant plant.
The first building, the west wing, was completed in the winter of
1903-04, on ground which had been unoccupied previously. It was
427 feet long and contained 88,000 square feet of floor space.

he demolition of the old front building was started in
arch 1904, and its replacement was completed in 1906.
he picture was taken at the dedication. (The clock hadn't
en installed.) It was 569 feet long and contained 116,000
square feet of floor space. The new buildings were equipped
with elevators and automatic telephone system. A power
plant was constructed in 1905-06.

During the administration of Charles H. Hulburd, Elgin's third president, 1898-1924, wage scales were improved, the working day was shortened, a pension system was established, and employees were given the opportunity to buy the company's stock. President Hulburd spent much of his time at the factory, conversing with employees, instead of remaining at the Chicago office.

Women workers predominate in this picture taken of the escape department in 1926. In November of that year, the company employed 4,370—2,200 women and 2,170 men. It was estimated that at least two-thirds of the employees were shareholders. Employee holdings ranged from one share to as high as fifty.

The Golden Stairway over the Milwaukee Road tracks was erected in 1923 for the benefit of employees who lived on the west side. They were often delayed in getting to work on time by freight trains halting to take on water. It was also used by small boys as a convenient perch to cast stones upon the trains beneath. The crossing was seldom blocked after locomotives were serviced at Spaulding, and the stairway was removed in 1935.

The hands of a woman operator are shown assembling jewels into balance cocks. The screws, adjacent to her rings, have perfect slots and threads as small as 360 to an inch.

Hundreds of Elgin couples first met on the job at the watch factory. "Archie Hill of the escape, and Miss Minnie Davis, of the balance, were matrimonialized at Lake Geneva last Saturday," reported the *Elgin Every Saturday* on August 30, 1890. "Mr. and Mrs. Hill have resumed factory duties amid the hearty congratulations of friends and acquaintances."

The operator is placing the balance and hairspring in the watch. Technical advances by the thirties made possible on accuracy standard of three one-hundred-thousandths of an inch. Assembling minute parts required painstaking concentration. Wages were usually based on piecework, and the tasks were often repetitive.

Delicate touch and exceptional dexterity were necessary in assembling miniature parts with accuracy. Watch hairsprings were so small that operators used microscopes as they attached them to balance wheels.

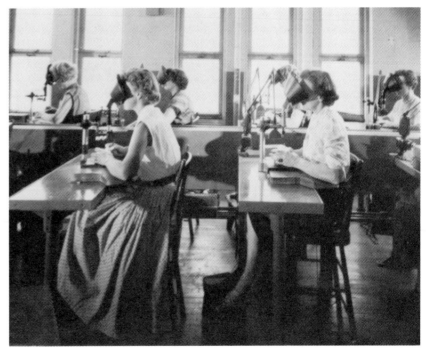

The clock tower was 144 feet high, with a fifty-three-foot flagpole topping it off. The big Seth Thomas clock had a gravity escapement and was regulated by a pendulum rod fourteen feet long on the end of which was a 330-pound weight. It was fitted with a switch to automatically light the dials. At night the time could be read from distances as far as half a mile.

This was the first self-winding tower clock ever put into operation when it began ticking on August 15, 1905. Each of the four dials were 14-1/2 feet in diameter and each minute hand was more than seven feet long.

Artistic license was taken in this often reproduced drawing of the watch factory (photo below). Not only were the fences along National Street and the buildings on the west side of South Grove Avenue omitted, but the length of the plant was magnified by adding twelve window bays to the front. The distortion can be seen in a comparison with a frontal view photograph (right).

The new factory was completed with the construction of additional wings in 1921-1923 and 1926-1927, bringing the total floor space to about twenty-one acres.

An observatory on the northeast corner of Watch and Raymond streets, opened in 1910, housed the instruments that timed Elgin watch movements to the stars. Elgin was the only watch manufacturer in America which maintained its own observatory. In every room of the nearby factory where movements were regulated was a sounding device telling the seconds. Each of these factory instruments was wired directly to the mean time clock in the observatory.

Star-fixed time started the New York Central's *Twentieth Century* train on its initial eighteen-hour run from Chicago to New York in 1932. At Chicago's Century of Progress Exposition in both 1933 and 1934, gates were opened daily by a time impulse from the observatory. Switchboard operators at the main plant gave the correct Elgin star time for an average of more than 500 callers daily from 1938 to 1955.

Two of the observatory's four clocks were in an underground room built of solid concrete. One was kept at "star" time, while the other was kept at standard railroad time for the nineteenth meridian. Constant temperature and air pressure was maintained by enclosing them in glass cylinders. Inside each case was a thermometer and a barometer.

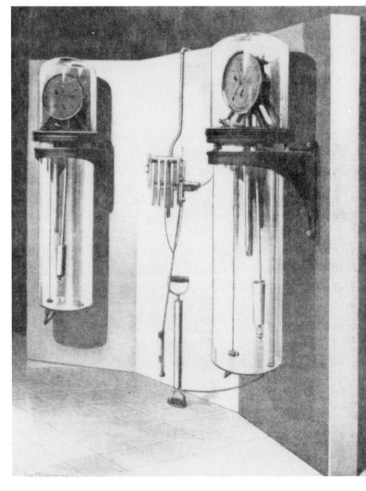

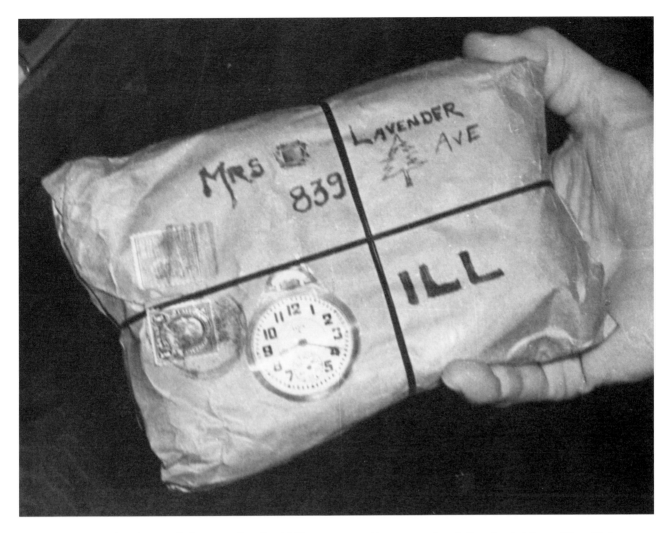

So famed was Elgin's watch factory that in 1939 the post office had no difficulty delivering this package to an address on Cedar Avenue. In the ragtime era a bordello pianist from New Orleans wrote a song entitled, "I've Got Elgin Movements in My Hips with a 20-year Guarantee."

The 50th millionth watch, a 21-jewel, 15/O size movement, was completed in 1951. All plates were gold plated. The dial was sterling silver with applied 18-karat gold markers. The hour, minute, and second hands were of solid gold. It was enclosed in an eighteen-karat natural gold case.

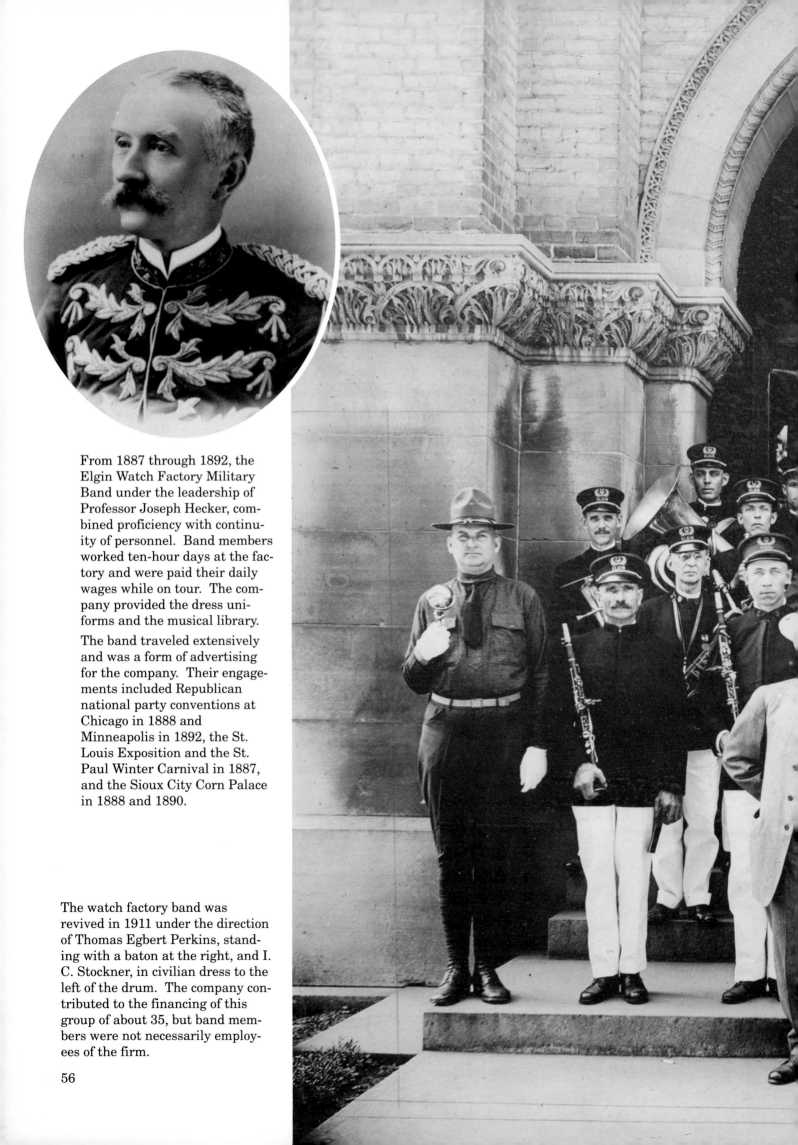

From 1887 through 1892, the Elgin Watch Factory Military Band under the leadership of Professor Joseph Hecker, combined proficiency with continuity of personnel. Band members worked ten-hour days at the factory and were paid their daily wages while on tour. The company provided the dress uniforms and the musical library.

The band traveled extensively and was a form of advertising for the company. Their engagements included Republican national party conventions at Chicago in 1888 and Minneapolis in 1892, the St. Louis Exposition and the St. Paul Winter Carnival in 1887, and the Sioux City Corn Palace in 1888 and 1890.

The watch factory band was revived in 1911 under the direction of Thomas Egbert Perkins, standing with a baton at the right, and I. C. Stockner, in civilian dress to the left of the drum. The company contributed to the financing of this group of about 35, but band members were not necessarily employees of the firm.

56

Elgin Watchmakers College, Elgin, Ill.

The Elgin Watchmakers College was established by the Elgin National Watch Co. in 1920. It was administered as a separate institution, but students had the advantage of the factory's technical facilities. More than 5,000 came to learn how to repair watches and clocks before the school closed in 1960.

In addition to repairing, the curriculum included machine engraving, stone setting, ring sizing and retail sales training. Many of the graduates became owners of jewelry stores. Graduates were prepared to take examinations set up by the Horological Institute or by states that required them. More students from the Elgin Watchmakers College passed these tests than did those from any other school.

During the Second World War, the Elgin National Watch Co. produced mechanical time fuses, field and navigation watches, timing devices, altimeter parts, stop watches, and elapsed time clocks. In 1943-44 soldiers, pictured below, enrolled at the Elgin Watchmakers College to learn how to repair watches in the field.

DESTRUCTION

In 1965 the main plant, termed by management as obsolete, and the Watchmakers College building were old. The abandoned factory was opened to the public for the sale of fixtures late that year, and many former workers took a sad last walk through empty work rooms.

A wrecking company began razing the building in the early summer of 1966, working from the back toward the front. One by one the sections fell, until only the clock tower remained. Then, on Sunday morning, October 3rd, dynamite charges brought the landmark crashing down into a pile of bricks, mortar, and twisted metal.

The watch industry was one of the first in America to succumb to foreign competition. Elgin is no longer a Watch City. Receding into a dimming past are memories of the clock tower, the bustling pay days, the shop talk, and the social events at the National House.

In an effort to reduce production costs, a new watch assembly plant was opened in 1963 in Blaney, South Carolina. The town was so eager to have the new factory, it changed its name to Elgin. In 1967-68, however, the firm phased out manufacturing in the United States.

59

THE WATCH FACTORY CLOCK

Merrill O. Calame

Among the things I've learned to love
        In friendship's interlock
Is that bright face that beams above—
        The old watch factory clock.

For years he's shone above the town,
        At night, by day, and all
And somehow wears a sort of crown
        Atop his tower tall.

When boyhood's lingering, careless pace
        Meant school might find me late
His hands asprawl across his face
        Would wave to speed my gait.

And courting days he played his part
        In stringing Cupid's tune,
When clouds would hinder lovers' art
        He'd fill in for the moon.

And when the rare bad times would come
        When he must have repair
The town faced pandemonium
        To find him off up there.

He sits upon the throne of space
        To guide our ways anon,
I'll always seek my old friend's face,
        And others—When I'm gone.

(Merrill O. Calame, an Elgin native, was a reporter for both the *Daily Courier* and the *Daily News* and later served as the Elgin Township assessor.)

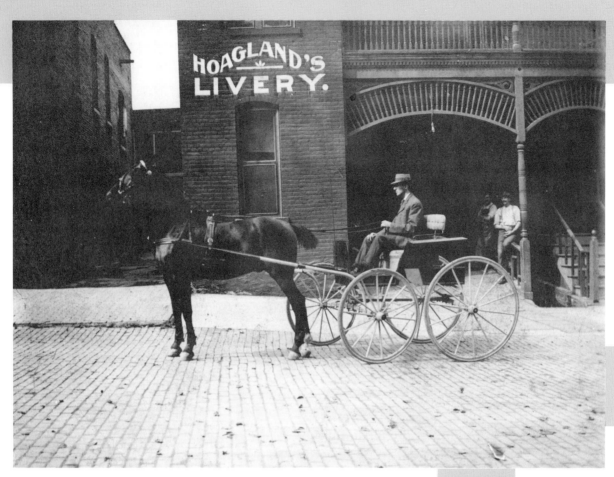

Most families could n[ot] afford to own a horse and rig. When needed they could be rented from a livery. Sam Hoagland opened his stable in 1880; by the time he retired in 191[ ] he owned twenty-six horses, eleven full-siz[e] closed carriages, thre[e] hearses, and a variety of fancy conveyances, opera hacks, pallbeare[r] wagons, and one-seat light driving rigs.

4

Ground transportation in Elgin progressed from horse power to railroads and streetcars to motor vehicles. They all rolled on wheels, and photographs record the sequence.

Horses were everywhere in 19th century Elgin. They pulled the wagons, buses and fire apparatus, and they had a big following at the Driving Park Association's harness racing track. And then in 1899 came an event that signaled a new era. "A four wheeled motorcycle, run by a gasoline engine" arrived from Evanston en route to Rockford. "The outfit created much comment as it sped along, accompanied by a bevy of cyclists," reported the *Elgin Daily News*. "Horse teams that were met scarcely knew what manner of thing it was, drawn by an invisible horse and they plunged about more or less."

For more than twenty-five years A. C. Muntz operated horse-drawn buses carrying watch workers to and from their homes. Before pavements were laid, there were times when the horses had to pull through seas of mud. Two teams to a bus were often necessary. Muntz, who founded what is now Elgin Warehouse and Equipment, gave up his last route in 1916.

Horses could haul heavy loads, such as cement building blocks for John McBride's Elgin Concrete and Structural Co. The wagons are stopped at the corner of Grove Avenue and South Spring Street in this photograph taken about 1910.

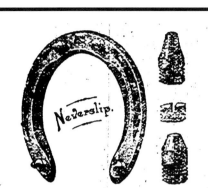
A number of businesses were based on the horse. The 1892 city directory listed fifteen livery, sale and boarding stables; fifty-six teamsters and expressmen; three trainers; seven harness shops; eight carriage and wagon makers; five shoers; and one breeder, as well as several feed suppliers. One of the blacksmiths was English-born William Tidmarsh, pictured in the doorway with one of his customers. One of the harness makers was John Spiess, whose shop was located on River Street.

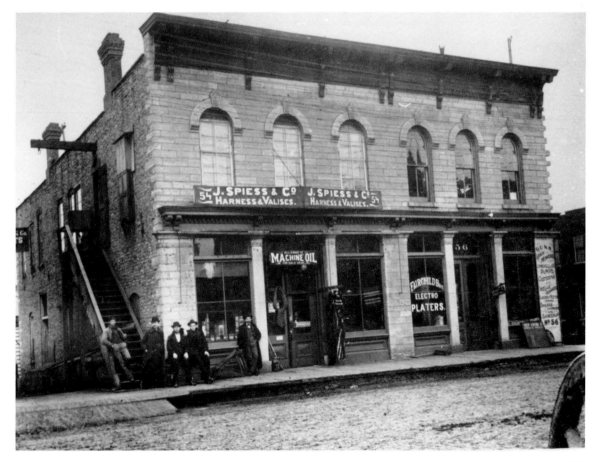

Horse-drawn milk wagons, like Charles F. Hawker's left the barns early in the morning because the lower temperature kept the milk from spoiling. Familiar sounds to light sleepers were the creaking of steel-rimmed wheels against the pavement and the clip-clop of the horse's hooves. An experienced animal would continue pulling the wagon, and even turn at the right corners, while the milkman was delivering the bottles to the steps of homes along the route. Hawker's, one of Elgin's smaller dairies, was in operation for forty years until Mr. Hawker retired in 1938.

A horse-drawn streetcar line began running on Grove avenue between the watch factory and Fountain Square in 1878. The tracks were later extended up Douglas and Dundee avenues. The horsecars were a disappointment. Citizens complained about the slow ride, poor track maintenance, and occasional abuse of the animals.

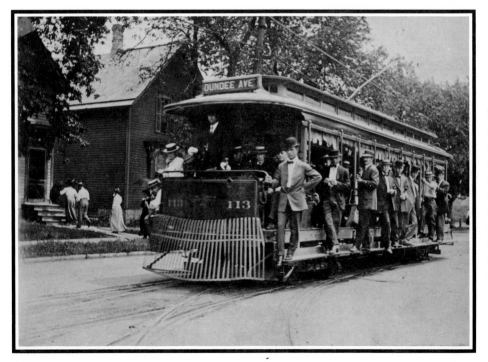

The Dundee Avenue streetcar could accommodate several gentlemen on its runningboards. Open-air cars such as the one shown were used during fair weather, but even then passengers had the option of lowering screens to protect against sudden rains or the hot sun.

The Elgin City Railway bought the horsecar franchise and began running electric cars on July 4, 1890. Within a year it had thirteen miles in operation. Construction crews are shown, at left, laying rails on South State Street. The picture below was taken about 1896 before the local firm was merged into an interurban trolley running through the Fox valley from Carpentersville on the north to Yorkville on the south.

The interurban trolley and streetcar lines in Elgin and Aurora were consolidated with the Aurora, Elgin & Chicago third rail in 1906. Bus service replaced streetcars on the unprofitable North State and Wing Park lines in 1931, and all streetcar service in Elgin ended on November 17, 1934. One of the buses of the succeeding Elgin City Lines, a private firm, is shown at the South Grove garage in 1938.

The Aurora, Elgin & Chicago electric interur ban began scheduled runs between Elgin and Wheaton in 1903 and established through se: vice to downtown Chicago in 1905. The line carried commuters and shoppers.
Recreational use on Sundays was also signifi cant. A reorganization in 1922 brought a change in name to Chicago, Aurora & Elgin. From this new title arose the popular designa tion, "Roarin' Elgin."

Car No. 204 of the Elgin & Belvidere Electric is turning into Chicago Street for its trip west (photo below). The 36.4-mile interurban, which began operating in 1907, used the tracks of the local streetcar line within the city. Headquarters and shops were in Marengo. The E&BE terminal on Grove avenue (photo above) was shared with the Aurora, Elgin & Chicago. The cars stopped at every crossroad and at some farm houses. Growing auto- mobile traffic reduced fares, and service ended in 1930.

Power for the AE&C was transmitted by a "hot" thir rail except when using loca streetcar tracks. The cur- rent was generated by a plant at Batavia which als provided electric light and power service for the city o Elgin. Revenues dropped with the spread of automo- bile ownership, and passen ger service ended in 1957.

In a time when the automobile, truck and airline are dominant means of transportation, it is difficult to conceive the significance railroads once had in the life of the community. In 1926, for example, twelve eastbound and twelve west bound passenger trains passed through the city daily on the Milwaukee. The west side North Western sent three trains in each direction between Chicago and Freeport, and the east side North Western was running three trains in each direction between Chicago and Williams Bay, Wisconsin.

Each day twenty-three interurban trolleys left for Aurora and thirty for Carpentersville on the Aurora, Elgin & Fox River Electric. Nine cars left daily for Belvidere on the Elgin, Belvidere & Electric, and twenty-four left for Chicago on the Chicago, Aurora & Elgin.

In addition to the four train stations downtown, the two steam lines and the 'Roarin' Elgin maintained "watch factory" stations near the big plant on the south end.

Freight business on the two steam lines, incoming and outgoing, amounted to nearly 25,000 car loads annually.

The west side depot of the "high" North Western near South Crystal Street, erected in 1869, was one of the line's oldest stations until it was razed in 1971.

When the Galena & Chicago Union (now the Chicago & North Western) came up along the river from South Elgin in 1849-50, the tracks crossed Poplar Creek south of town on a pile trestle. It was replaced, possibly in 1860-61, by this two-arched masonry viaduct. It is the oldest existing "bridge" in the Elgin area.

The Chicago & Pacific railroad arrived in 1873 to break the North Western's monopoly, but it was soon in receivership. The Chicago, Milwaukee, St. Paul & Pacific, which became known as the Milwaukee Road, secured control of the stock in 1880. An impressive new passenger station was erected in Elgin the following year. It was razed for a replacement in 1947.

About forty years made a big difference in the Milwaukee locomotives. Above is an engine in the Elgin yard about the turn of the century. Below is a Class S2 locomotive pulling out of Elgin in 1939. Across the river is the business district.

The Milwaukee Road's streamliner, the *Hiawatha*, began running through Elgin between Chicago and Omaha in 1940. Pulled by an oil-burning locomotive capable of speeds of more than a mile a minute, the train included a tap-room, diner, parlor cars, a lounge-observation car, and luxury coaches—all air-conditioned. It stopped in Elgin for passengers with reservations.

Elgin's first automobile, a red Waverly Electric, was purchased by George Richardson, superintendent of the David C. Cook Publishing Co., in October 1900. It ran on four one-horse batteries and could be driven thirty miles after charging. There were four rates of speed, from three to sixteen miles per hour. Richardson drove the car three years before he purchased a three-cylinder Thomas Flyer.

On July 13, 1906 a cornerstone was laid at what is now St. Paul's United Church of Christ. Pictured are two automobiles and two horse-drawn carriages. The cars had leather license tags issued by the city. The automobile in the center was a light steam car. The one on the left was a Marr "Autocar," produced in Elgin by the Fauber Manufacturing Co.

Sam Hoagland's son, Fred joined the business after leaving high school. When the livery closed, he adapted to the motor age, purchased a bus, and started the Hoagland Taxicab Co. with three Model T Fords and two Reos.

With the increasing number of automobiles on the city's streets, the Elgin Motor Club was organized in 1912, when there were about 500 locally-owned vehicles. The club's primary objective was to get its members' cars out of the mire and onto a network of good roads. It pressured township road commissioners to improve their highways, erected directional and cautionary signs, distributed travel information, and provided mechanical first aid.

Members of the Elgin Motor Club and other volunteers are conducting one of their do-it-yourself projects, removing rocks and debris from what is now Highway 19 east of the city. Since they aren't dressed in "work" clothes, the picture, taken in 1913, was especially posed for the photographer.

Born in Sweden, Charles J. Moody built two or three cars in his machine shop on River Street. It was in the same building which once housed the harness shop of John Spiess. Donald S. Hubbell's Ford dealership moved next door in 1914.

The Elgin Storage and Transfer Co. of A. C. Muntz bought its first motor truck in 1915, and by 1920 was operating thirteen ranging in capacity from one to five tons. By then the firm's trucks outnumbered horse-drawn wagons.

Originally a stable, the Coliseum at 116 South Grove was later used as a movie theater, roller rink and dance hall before it was sold to A. C. Muntz in 1915 for conversion to a garage. It was wrecked by an explosion and fire in 1924, rebuilt, and razed for a parking lot in 1974.

5

When James Gifford first platted his town, Center Street, above the often flooded lowland along the river, was to be the heart of the business district. The river mills, however, soon attracted stores, and when the city government was incorporated in 1864, the mid-point of its four-square mile area was the intersection of what are now East Chicago Street and Grove and Douglas avenues. To this place farmers brought produce, wood and livestock for sale to merchants, and it became known as Market Square.

A Liberty Pole was erected in 1864 at what would become a focal point for community celebrations and ceremonies. A two-tier cast iron fountain and horse-watering tank was installed in the Square—really a triangle—in 1873. The water was piped from "Borden's Springs" near the corner of North Street and Douglas Avenue. Market Square then became Fountain Square. "The water in these fountains is of the best quality." was a contemporary description, but it was responsible for mud puddles in the vicinity when heavy winds sent a spray upon the unpaved streets. The fountain was removed in 1903.

On the north end of the Square, where Philo Patterson once had a little grocery store and garden patch, Orlando Davidson erected his Home Bank Block in 1860. His bank, its notes backed by seceding Southern states, failed in 1861. It was re-established with a state charter. Davidson, James T. Gifford's son-in-law, became the first president of the Home National Bank when it was organized in 1872.

The building was purchased by Henry Lee Borden, a son of Gail Borden, in 1881, and he immediately began an extensive remodeling. The entire building was raised three feet, and a basement placed under the structure. Another story and a mansard roof were added. It then became known as the Borden Block.

Elgin's first hydraulic passenger elevator was installed in 1886-87. The operator, it was announced, made 760 trips on March 22, 1897.

Borden sold the building to the Home National Bank in 1890. It was razed in 1928 for construction of the bank's Tower building.

Town's Block, first erected in 1851, housed Morris Clinton Town's Bank of Elgin until it defaulted in the financial panic of 1857. Located on the southeast corner of the Square, it was destroyed in the fire of 1874 and quickly rebuilt as shown here. Stores were on the ground floor, and offices were upstairs.

Another fire, in 1879, again badly damaged Town's Block and consumed two stores and several offices. All the Elgin Board of Trade records were destroyed. For a time it was feared that the corner and walls of the ruins would fall. The building was again rebuilt, substantially as it appears here. The Odd Fellows met here for more than fifty years, and Town's was at one time the quarters for the YMCA. The main floor was occupied by the Union National Bank beginning in 1904. It was torn down by the bank in 1960 for a new building.

This was known as McNeil's Corner on the Square. Malcolm and John McNeil, brothers who were born in Scotland, moved their grocery to the northwest corner of Chicago and River streets in 1866. They left for Chicago in 1872 to become two of the partners in a wholesale grocery business, McNeil & Higgins.

The Elgin National Bank, organized in 1892, occupied this building on the northwest corner of North Grove and East Chicago beginning in 1895. A new bank building was erected on the site in 1967-68.

William G. Hubbard, a pioneer merchant, established a store on the northeast corner of Chicago Street and Douglas Avenue in 1851. It was occupied by John Newman when it was destroyed by the great fire of March 1874. The white brick building that replaced it that year was connected, on the second and third floors, with the adjoining block. The building shown here was torn down in 1909 and replaced by a new block, financed by Hubbard's son, the following year. It was called the Lawyers Building when it was gutted by fire in 1979 and leveled in 1980.

This is the west side of the triangular Square as it appeared in the early seventies before the pump and liberty pole were replaced by a fountain. At the left is the DuBois Opera House. In the center, beyond the pole, is the Bosworth Block. Adjacent to the north is the First National Bank, and at the extreme right is a corner of Davidson's bank.

The Square was paved with cedar blocks in 1891; proving unsatisfactory, they were replaced with bricks. The arc light tower and fountain, at the left of the picture, were removed in 1903, although the triangle continued to be called Fountain Square. A fountain was restored in 1967.

A popcorn and peanut stand was a fixture on Fountain Square for about fift years. Started by Jim Morrison, it wa taken over by Carl Bloemke in 1909. year later Ernest (Buster) Brown became his partner. Willis Brown, Ernest's brother, purchased Bloemke's interest in 1919.

The Browns operated the concession seven days a week from 8 a.m. to 10 p.m. until they retired in 1958. Annu output of popcorn reached a peak of te tons. The oak and copper stand had several dents caused by bricks hurled through the air during the Palm Sunday tornado of 1920. What happened to the stand? It was last seen baking in an Arizona desert in 1968.

This is how the Square looked in 1966. The Osco drug store has taken the place of the Opera House. The site is now a parking lot. A 65-foot flagpole was erected by the American Legion in 1940.

BUSY STREETS

Grove Avenue from Prairie Street north to the Square, now part of a pedestrian mall, was once the busiest thoroughfare in town. It has provided access over the years to movie houses, a hotel, the post office, banks, a restaurant, bowling alley and billiard parlor, groceries, a department store, clothing shops, an automobile dealership, a florist, druggists, and five and tens. It was the first street to be paved with asphalt, in 1903, and when electric streetlights were installed in 1922, Mayor Price called it Elgin's "great white way."

A wood sidewalk is a dominant feature in this view of the west side of Grove Avenue photographed about 1873 from the DuPage Street intersection. Bruce Payne's livery stable is at the extreme left. Next door is Arwin Price's monument works. The two large structures are the Opera House, built in 1870, and further north, Bosworth Brothers & Peck ("dry goods, notions, oil cloths, live geese feathers, and furs").

The same street in 1910 was paved and serviced by electric streetcars. Parked in front of the Elgin Fruit and Candy Co.'s ice cream parlor is a Coca-Cola delivery truck. The three-story building in the center, once Bosworth's store, is now occupied by Ike Cohien's women's and children's wear store. Bay windows have been added. The adjacent columned building was the First National Bank.

By 1954 buses had replaced streetcars on Grove Avenue, and the Rialto Theater occupied the site formerly occupied by the Opera House. Overhead wires have been removed, and TV antennas are visible. A traffic light now dominates the right side of the picture.

Industries once flourished in close proximity to the Square. This is a view looking south on River Street. Gronberg, Bierman & Co. completed the big three-story brick building, at the right of the picture, in 1870. It was later occupied for more than forty years by the Western Casket Hardware Co., which became Elgin Metal Casket. The Elgin Iron Works, which also started up in 1870, was a short-lived producer of sewing machine stands and steam engines.

The Fox River separates the west side from the east side; Chicago Street is the dividing line between north and south. In the first photograph, probably made in 1866, the street is unpaved. The large home of Drs. Henry and Susan (Daggett) Whitford, topped by a cupola, is in the right foreground at the northwest corner of Center and Chicago streets. He opened an Elgin office in 1857, and she received her diploma in 1871. In the center of the picture, on the north side of the street, is Shaw's hotel.

The Whitford flats, completed in 1887, have replaced the Whitford home in this view of East Chicago Street from the Center Street crossing. They were purchased by the YWCA, next door, in 1918 for use as a women's dormitory. Towering above the other buildings on the north side of the street is the city hall. The bay-windowed building at the extreme left was erected in 1892 and is still standing.

It is now 1937 and cars are parked along downtown Chicago Street. The skyscraper is the Elgin Tower, and the narrow Hubbard Block is across the street. Roveltad's jewelry store, a family enterprise through four generations, occupied the same Chicago Street location from 1893 until it closed its doors in 1959.

STORES AND LANDMARKS

Downtown was a place to shop, go to the po[st] office, visit professional offices, take in a vaudeville [or] picture show, and perhaps drop in at the library. F[or] men there were saloons, billiard parlors, and barbe[r] shops. Some of the buildings, often ornate and of va[r]ied architectural styles, became familiar landmarks.

George M. Peck became a store partner with the Bosworth brothers in 1868. A few years later he sold his interest and purchased a grocery and dry goods business in the Opera House Block. A fire in 1886 scattered the business into five locations. He purchased the old city hall on Grove Avenue and completed this building on the site in 1893. It was blown apart in the Palm Sunday tornado of 1920.

When Peck's department store was destroyed in the tornado, he authorized construction of a new building on the site. Before it was completed, however, he sold out to Joseph Spiess, who moved into the new store on February 8, 1921. This explains why Peck's name appears at the top of the building in this 1948 photograph. The store was doubled in size with an addition, and new facade, completed in 1950, and in 1969 the firm expanded again by acquiring the adjacent S. S. Kresge building. The store was removed to the Spring Hill Mall in 1981.

When William D. Ackemann announced the grand opening of his new department store in 1895, most of the "departments" were actually smaller businesses renting space. The location on Milwaukee Street (now East Highland Avenue) was thought to be too far from the Square to attract many customers, but the business quickly grew. Before the turn of the century, "W. D." brought four brothers into the firm. This photograph shows the store after a third floor was added in 1898. Ackemann's eventually expanded to cover the entire plot from the North Western tracks east to Spring Street and from East Highland north to Division. In 1985 the store was sold to new owners specializing in home furnishings.

Theodore F. Swan opened a grocery in 1867; by 1880 he had broadened his offerings to include dry goods and shoes. Swan was the first Elgin merchant to install a railway system to send money from any part of the store to the cashier. Unlike many other stores, sales were strictly cash. After Theodore F. Swan died, the business was carried on by his son, Theodore I. Swan. Swan's occupied this building from 1908 until the firm closed its doors in 1938. It was then leased by Sears, Roebuck until leaving for the Spring Hill Mall in 1980. Elgin Community College opened its downtown extension here in 1983.

Born in Germany, August Scheele became a partner in a basement grocery in 1884. By 1902 he had erected his own building at the northwest corner of Douglas Avenue and Division Street. An addition in 1910 doubled its size. In 1920 Scheele's had eight vehicles making deliveries to any part of the city. Of the 55 employees, four were assigned solely to taking orders over the telephone. A meat department was added in 1926. The largest food store in Elgin, its trade extended over a wide area. The business was sold to outside interests in 1936 and closed in 1944.

Meat markets had sawdust on the floor and sausages dangling from the ceiling. Carcasses hung from hoists or big hooks. Liver and bones for dogs were given away. Leitner Brothers was located on the southeast corner of Chicago and Spring streets.

In 1904 the Leitners erected a three-story brick building on their lot. At the right of the picture is Stewart's Hall, once known as the Academy of Music. It was completed in 1888. Both buildings are still standing.

A Belgian immigrant, Nick Goedert, became a saloon proprietor in 1884. His establishment wasn't typical. There was no free lunch, for example, and no cash register. He obeyed the liquor laws to the letter. There was no "just one more drink" after the closing hour. No minors were served, and no gambling was allowed. Singing and boisterous behavior were discouraged. A patron who appeared to be inebriated was asked to leave. Goedert's saloon, a local institution for more than thirty years, closed in 1914 when the township was voted dry in a local option referendum.

James Lewis, pictured in action behind the bar, was Goedert's bartender for twenty-five years.

During the years 1884-1902 the post office was located in the Hunter and Hawkins building at the northeast corner of DuPage Street and South Grove Avenue. The building was razed in 1941 for the construction of a Woolworth store.

The first building to be erected exclusively for postal purposes was opened in 1902 and enlarged by additions in 1910 and 1928. It was vacated in 1966, when a new post office opened in 1966. After the building was demolished in 1969, the site became what is now Carleton Rogers Park on North Spring Street between East Highland Avenue and Division Street.

In its early days the post office was a hangout for gentlemen of leisure. "I was up to the post office this morning," complained a woman to the weekly *Advocate* in 1904, and the sidewalks and steps were covered with slime, tobacco juice and filth." A spitting contest had been held there the previous evening.

This was the first Elgin building to be equipped with a revolving door.

Mail delivery service within the city was introduced in 1884 with one letter carrier at $850 per annum and four auxiliary carriers at $600 each per annum. Rural free delivery was begun in 1903. The picture of the carriers was taken in 1897.

The brick residence of David Scofield on Spring Street, built in the early seventies, was purchased in 1892 by Alfred B. Church and Samuel M. Church and donated to Elgin Township for use as a library. They stipulated that it be named the Gail Borden Public Library in memory of their stepfather. Extensive remodeling, which included the addition of the two wings, was carried out under the direction of W. W. Abell, an architect who was also responsible for the Spurling Block. The formal opening came on February 22, 1894.

The building was abandoned for a new structure in the Civic Center in 1968. It was later fitted out as an extension of Ackemann's department store and in 1985 was converted to restaurant use.

In contrast to the simplicity of modern design, the business "blocks" of an earlier Elgin were ornamented. The News-Advocate's quarters on the southwest corner of Spring and Chicago streets featured rounded arches and a turreted roof. It was build in 1894 partially from lumber and other materials salvaged from the Chicago world's fair. Abandoned by the *Daily News* after its merger with the *Daily Courier* in 1925, the building was razed for a parking lot in 1974.

Elgin's first steel-framed building was erected by Col. Andrew Spurling in 1892-93 at the northwest corner of DuPage and South Spring streets. The facades were of pressed brick with terra cotta and copper trim. Besides professional offices, the occupants have included a bowling alley, the Swan department store, 1894-1908, and the *Elgin Daily Courier-News*, 1926-1956. Crowds once gathered along the Spring Street side to read posted results of sporting events and election returns. Originally the Spurling had an overhanging cornice. The bay windows were reduced and replaced by windows of aluminium and a glass curtain wall when the building was remodeled in 1957 and renamed the Elgin Commerce Building.

The McBride Block, 53-61 Douglas Avenue, erected in 1889, had a balcony, a bay window, elaborate finials, and a decorated gable. All this disappeared in 1970 when the facade was covered with metal sheathing.

n the west side of South Grove, at what would ow be 56-58, Leopold Adler and his son-in-law, braham Strauss, erected in 1889 a three story and asement commercial building. The second floor rved at various times as a ballroom, concert hall, ymnasium, and National Guard armory. It was lso an arena for boxing and wrestling matches. he Elgin Board of Trade met in the Adler-Strauss lock, 1891-1907. The building was torn down in 956 and replaced by a Walgreen drug store.

The Sherwin Block, erected in 1902 on the site of Shaw's hotel at the northwest corner of Spring and Chicago, continued the interest in ornament into the twentieth century. Note the triangular window overhangs and the decorative work between the second and third floors. The Sherwin was razed in 1957.

HOTELS

Long before motels with swimming pools and cable TV arose along the highways, downtown hotels were a vibrant part of the city's life. Their runners met travelers arriving by train and offered free transportation to their rooms. By an early ordinance, each hotel was limited to two runners, and they were prohibited from using abusive language on any visitors who selected a rival hotel. Other guests were semi-permanent boarders, many of them newly-employed watch workers. The larger hotels provided a sample room for the traveling salesman, a bar for the thirsty, a dining room for the hungry and a stable for those needing a rig.

The Nolting House, opened late in 1882 on the southeast corner of DuPage Street and Grove Avenue, was a reconstruction of the former Bluff City Hotel which had been built in the seventies. One of the Elgin bands used to rehearse at the Nolting. Guests enjoyed listening to the music and sitting out on the balcony, enclosed with a wrought iron fencing. John L. Sullivan, the world heavyweight boxing champion, once stayed at the Nolting. The Nolting was converted into a store and office building in 1887 and was razed for a J. C. Penney store in 1937.

The Western, still standing on North State Street near West Highland Avenue, was probably built in the seventies. Charley Mackh enlarged and remodeled the building in 1880, adding the mansard roof and ornamenting the railing with "Western House" in letters twenty-seven inches high.

Four years later he provided an early form of air-conditioning by installing a huge fan in the basement that pushed cool air through the hallways. Rooms at the Western were $1 per day in the eighties, a rate that may have contributed to the demise of the more sumptuous Waverly across the street.

ected in 1887-88 on the west side of Grove
enue, the Kelley was a three-story brick struc-
re which extended 180 feet toward the river.
e lower floor was occupied by stores and a
loon, while the thirty rooms in the upper sto-
s were fitted out in elegant style. A canopy
ich extended out over the sidewalk served as
eviewing stand for parades which passed
rough the business district.

e Kelley enjoyed heavy patronage from the-
rical companies performing at the Opera
use next door and leading figures of the auto-
obile industry during the Elgin Road Races.
e visitor, however, was disgusted. Carry A.
ation, who became a celebrity by breaking up
loons, came to town in 1909. "They directed
e to the Kelley house," she stormed. "I
uldn't sleep in a hotel which is connected with
saloon if I could help it—not unless I had to
ep in the street."

e canopy was removed in 1944. The hotel was
cated in 1971 after it failed to meet safety and fire
de standards. It was leveled the following year.

The Jennings House, erected in 1881-82
on the northwest corner of Douglas
Avenue and East Highland Avenue,
opened without a bar or billiard room, a
startling departure for its day. "The
guests who love quiet are not disturbed
by the clinking glasses and the noise of
revelry," reported the weekly *Advocate*
on December 22, 1883. The Jennings
occupied the second and third floors of a
commercial block. The building was
razed for the Civic Center development
in 1965.

Merchant, real estate subdivider, industrial promoter, and transit line developer, William E. Grote was a German immigrant who grasped the business opportunities abounding in Elgin's greatest period of expansion and became one of the city's greatest benefactors. An active Republican, he served two successive terms as mayor of Elgin, 1891-1895. A devout member of the German Evangelical Association, now Faith United Methodist Church, he donated one third the cost of erecting its big new building in 1893.

This was the last of the old grist mills along River Street, which was renamed North Grove Avenue in 1923. It replaced a frame building destroyed by fire in 1887. The Elgin Flour and Feed Co., incorporated in 1905, produced "Lady Elgin" flour and "Yellow Legged" chicken feed. Water wheels capable of generating 200 horsepower operated the machinery. The business closed in 1957 when the building was purchased by the city and razed for a parking lot.

6

"Factories have made Elgin," reported the *Quincy* (Illinois) *Journal*
1891, "and the businessmen have spent money lavishly in order to get
ese factories."

Taking advantage of the industrial unrest in Chicago and of Elgin's
:ation on two major rail lines, William E. Grote and his associates were
le to attract several firms and lessen the city's dependence upon the
itch factory. To persuade industries to remove to Elgin, he and his
rtners offered free land for a plant site, and on occasion even provided
puilding. Then they subdivided the land around the plant into lots for
le to employees.

The Elgin Packing Co., a vegetable cannery at West Chicago and Union streets,
began operations in time for the 1870 harvest. The plant was expanded over the
years until five buildings, some of them
three stories high, covered more than an
acre of ground. During the harvest season
from 200 to 500 men, women and children
were employed. A series of poor crop years
beginning in 1914 signalled the cannery's
decline. Production was finally halted in
the early twenties.

Daily output at the cannery rose to more
than 60,000 two-pound cans of corn with
the progressive introduction of improved
machinery. A million-can season wasn't
unusual. Skilled huskers could average
sixty to seventy-five bushels a day. In
the early years, to satisfy the needs of
large families, two- and three-pound cans
were standard.
Among the brand
names, besides
"Elgin Cream,"
were "Watch
Brand" and "Fox
River."

Cyrus H. Woodruff was one of the owners of a foundry established in 1867 to make fine quality castings for watch factory machinery. Later he moved his operations to South Elgin and then in 1879 erected an iron works parallel with the Chicago & Pacific (now Soo Line) tracks on Elgin's west side. The main output in the early years consisted of castings for school seats and desks and opera chairs. Woodruff & Edwards (Alfred Edwards purchased a half interest in 1900) received an Army-Navy E in 1944 for a round-the-clock production of landing craft propellers. The foundry was closed in 1987, and the buildings were demolished in 1990.

The Woodruff foundry began making large cast iron coffee mills for grocers, hotels and restaurants in 1889. They came in both counter top and floor models and were finished in red, blue and gold bronze colors. The largest weighed 365 pounds and could hold up to nine pounds of coffee for grinding. Production ceased in 1917 after a fire destroyed the molds.

1868 Casper Althen purchased an inter-
st in a local brewery on the west side of
e river above the dam and north of the
stillery. The firm was incorporated in
394. Until a bottling plant was erected in
398, all the beer was delivered in barrels
kegs. Adler Brau ("Eagle Beer") was a
pular brand in northern Illinois. The
ant, which occupied fourteen acres, was
osed in 1920, although bootleggers con-
nued to use its equipment until a spec-
cular raid by Prohibition agents in 1923.
he long abandoned, dilapidated buildings
ere leveled in 1963.

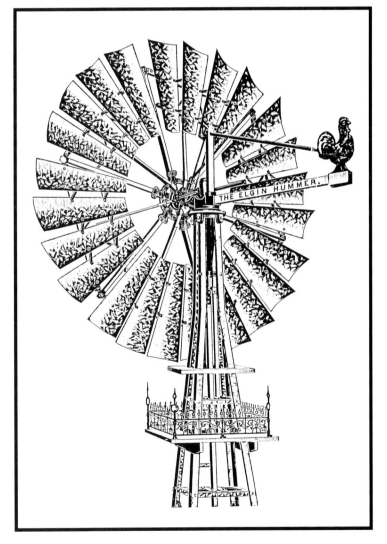

he name of the Elgin Wind Power and Pump Co., orga-
ized in 1887, was changed to the Elgin Windmill Co. in
25. Gilbert B. Snow, the plant manager, patented an
tomatic oiler in 1906. The entire gearing mechanism of
e Wonder model ran in a bath of oil. One gallon oiled the
ain shaft and all working parts for at least one year, elimi-
ating frequent and hazardous climbs up the tower. The
st profitable year was 1929, and the business was sold to
e Woodruff & Edwards foundry in 1943.

The Hummer, one of several models of the Elgin Wind
Power and Pump Co., was a vaneless open wheel mill especially adapted for use in low places and between buildings,
or high hills and trees where the currents of wind are very
unsteady. In a brisk pumping wind the Hummer made from
thirty to thirty-five revolutions per minute. The rooster
always faced the wind.

"THIS IS A GREAT BARGAIN, MA'AM!"

Seeing for Himself.

Tommy ran into the house from | the yard, where he was playing, for his top. As he opened the kitchen door, he found the baby screaming

David C. Cook, a young printer with a profound knowledg of the Bible, published his first lesson help, "Our Sunday School Quarterly," in 1875 for use in his own religion class es. While he was serving as superintendent of the Sunday School at Elgin's First Methodist Church, 1895-1925, it wa said to have the largest enrollment in the state.

In 1882 the David C. Cook Publishing Co., the world's largest producer of non-denominational Sunday School materials, moved its presses from Chicago to Elgin. The plant, originally located in the old woolen mill along the Fox River, was soon enlarged. At the end of the decade, Cook had completed the Marguerite Block on East Chicago Street, at the river's edge, employed 350 people, and was printing four weekly papers, one semi-monthly, ten monthlies and eighteen quarterlies.

The engraving shows the first home of the publishing house in Elgin.

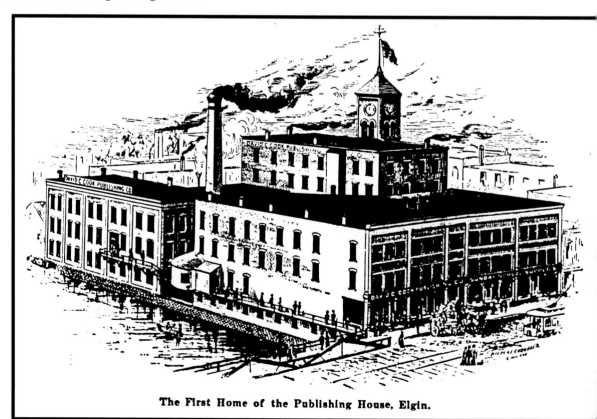

The First Home of the Publishing House, Elgin.

ecause the offices of the Elgin National
Watch Co. were located in Chicago, the David
C. Cook Publishing Co. employed more clerical
workers than any local industry. In 1913 the
firm was supplying more than 60,000 Sunday
schools with material. An average of fifteen
tons was sent out daily, aggregating more than
nine million pounds annually. The combined
annual circulation of some forty publications
exceeded 100,000,000.

The Cook firm had a major impact on the local
post office. The 1,102,461 pounds of printed
material sent out in 1888 accounted for 0.75
percent of all second-class mail in the United
States. In 1895 a postal clerk was stationed at
the plant to cancel the stamps.

Cook's removed its
operations to a new,
well-lighted building
in the north end in
1901. The plant,
expanded in 1907
and 1914, was on a
site that eventually
grew to thirteen
acres. The big
printer was the first
major industrial
firm in Elgin to
reduce the work day
to nine hours and
again led with an
eight-hour day in
1911.

The Elgin Silver Plate Co., a producer of casket hardware, started up in 1892. The first major industrial plant on the far west side, it was located on a block surrounded by Clifton and Melrose avenues and Carr and Erie streets. In 1902 the firm manufactured 1.2 million pounds of coffin hardware, nameplates, ornaments and cornices. It was acquired in 1926 by the Western Casket Hardware Co. The building was gutted by fire in 1972 before it was razed. The site is now occupied by single family homes.

In 1928 Western Casket began manufacturing caskets of various metals as well as the trimming. The most expensive were those finished in silver and bronze. The remains of Calvin Coolidge, 30th President of the United States, are buried in an Elgin-made casket. The name of the firm was changed to Elgin Metal Casket in 1939. Operations were removed to Richmond, Indiana, in 1982.

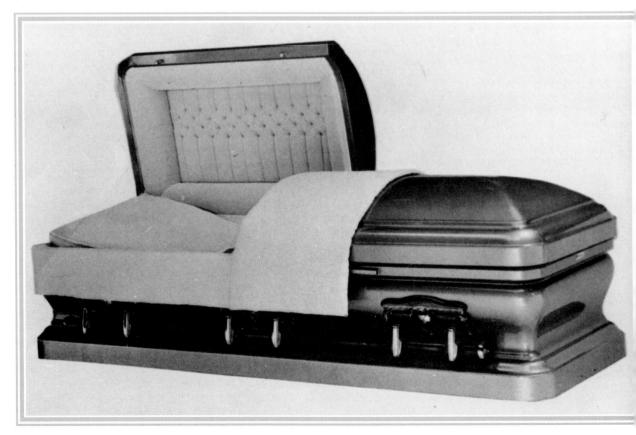

H. K. Cutter and C. H. Crossette moved their shirt factory from Chicago in 1892 in return for a three story brick building on the east side of North Liberty Street between Slade Avenue and Page Street. It was similar in design, although smaller, to the shoe factory.

In the mid-twenties most shirts had collars, unlike the one pictured in the 1896 advertisement. The firm was then producing about 250,000 broadcloth shirts annually with material imported from England. Colors were white, blue, tan and gray. The factory made its own cardboard boxes. Like several other Elgin industries, most of the employees were women. Cutter & Crossette closed in 1930, and the building was later occupied by a shoe factory. It was torn down and replaced by a supermarket in 1965.

The "case factory," not connected with the Elgin National Watch Co., was the city's second largest employer for more than forty years. The Illinois Watch Case Co. removed from Chicago in 1890. It was one of the industries encouraged to locate in Elgin by William Grote's efforts. The cases were of solid gold, silver, gold-filled, and silver and gold plated of all sizes. Decorative work was both hand engraved and stamped.

Besides watch cases, the company manufactured lockets, novelty jewelry, cigarette lighters, and vanity cases. During World War II the firm was a major producer of chemical mortar shells. Output in the big plant on Dundee avenue, hard hit by foreign competition, ended in the early sixties.

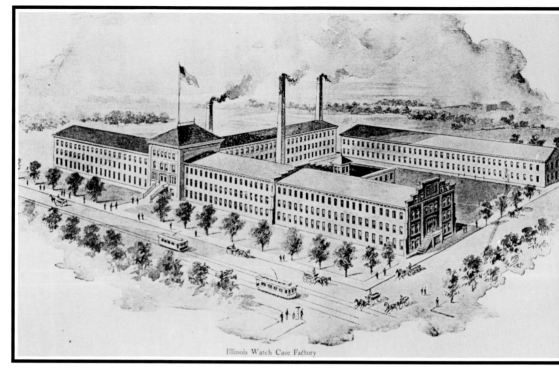

Illinois Watch Case Factory

A press with one operation cut and shaped the back of the watch case from long strips of metal. "This press is provided with dies of every description, size and shape; some with the various designs which ornament the back and front of the case," reported the *Elgin Weekly Courier*, July 12, 1890. "Thus it cuts from the sheet of gold the circular piece, shapes it and stamps upon it 'engraved' designs with one operation of the press. The work is so fine that none but an expert could tell the difference between the stamped and engraved work."

"Elgin Queen."   Price, $75.00.

The Elgin Cycle Co., a subsidiary of the Illinois Watch Case Co., was one of three local firms mass-producing bicycles during the nineties. Trade names were the "Elgin King" for men and "Elgin Queen" for women.

In the early days of the automobile, machine shops all over the country were making horseless carriages. The Elgin Sewing Machine & Bicycle Co., located in the Wright Avenue factory, in 1898 contracted with the American Electric Vehicle Co. of Chicago to build five "runabouts." These electrics, powered by twenty-eight storage batteries, were operable for fifty miles between charges and had a top speed of fourteen miles per hour. The wheels were bicycle wheels with metal rims and extra strong spokes. "It will climb hills without puffing and snorting, and it never balks or runs away," the advertising claimed, and "It isn't afraid of streetcars at all.

The Elgin Automobile Co. was another ill-fated venture at the Wright Avenue factory. About fifteen Winners were made in 1899-1900.

Henry F. VanWambeke and Sons constructed about eight "Van" delivery wagons in a barn behind their store at Hill and Jefferson streets during the years 1907-1909.

One and a half million bricks and 14,000 square feet of glass went into the construction of this factory on Wright Avenue near Bluff City Boulevard. It was erected in 1891 for the R. S. Dickie Manufacturing Co., a printer of can labels, show cards, and advertising novelties. The firm was in receivership about a month after presses first began turning. Succeeding producers of pneumatic signal and brake systems for trains, bicycles, and electric and gasoline automobiles were also failures in this ill-fated factory. A cyclone on May 25, 1896 tore apart the main structure. The plant was finally destroyed by fire on August 11, 1904.

The Church of the Brethren moved its publishing house from Mt. Morris to Elgin in 1899 and erected a three-story brick building on South State Street. An addition in 1906 extended the front with an arched opening into a court. The *Gospel Messenger*, the church's official paper, was printed here as well as Sunday School quarterlies, papers and leaflets. Besides its own publications, the plant also printed and bound school and song books on orders from publishers. The building was vacated in 1959 for new quarters in the northeast end of the city. It was consumed by a spectacular fire on September 25, 1991.

The Seybold Reed Pipe Organ Co. moved to Elgin from Chicago in 1903. Pianos were added to the line in 1908 and soon became the chief output. By 1913 Seybold was producing about 2,000 pianos annually. Many of these were player pianos. An ill-fated merger and the loss of much of its foreign market with the outbreak of war in Europe, forced the company into receivership in 1914. The vacant plant was acquired by another piano manufacturer, the E. P. Johnson Co., the following year.

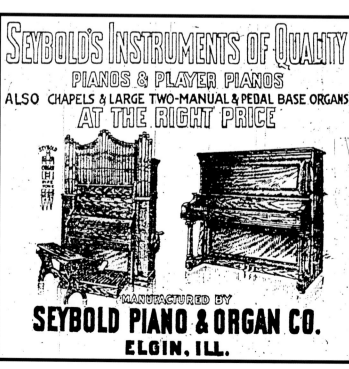

member the "tiny train" at the amusement park you
[ri]de when a child? Beginning in 1905 the International
[Mi]niature Railway Co. produced a twelve-inch gauge
[en]gine that could haul as many as six cars carrying
[tw]enty-four adults or forty-eight children. Including
[th]e tender, it was about eight feet long. International
[al]so made the cars. Because this was an Elgin indus-
[try], the proprietors could not resist advertising that the
[en]gine's parts were "as perfect in construction as a
[wa]tch." By the time the partnership dissolved in 1908,
[In]ternational had constructed more than 20 six-horse-
[po]wer engines. They were purchased by amusement
[pa]rks from San Francisco to Boston.

The Western Thread Co. of Chicago completed a
plant on Bluff City Boulevard in 1910. Albert
B. Collingbourne (the ABC on the spool box
shown at the left) acquired a controlling interest two years later. The firm, later called
Collingbourne Mills, produced millions of silk,
cotton and rayon spools as well as stamped
embroidery patterns. It went into the hands of
receivers in 1938.

[Th]e Van Sicklen Co. moved to Elgin from
[Au]rora in 1915, when a contract was signed
[wi]th the Elgin National
[W]atch Co. for the use of
[sp]ace in its big plant. At
[it]s peak in 1920, the firm
[em]ployed more than 500
[an]d was producing over a
[th]ousand instruments
[da]ily. The Van Sicklen
[sp]eedometer, "built like a
[wa]tch," calibrated an air
[cu]rrent and translated the
[re]sult into miles per hour.

[St]ewart-Warner purchased
[th]e Van Sicklen Co. in
[19]21 and continued opera-
[ti]ons in Elgin until 1924,
[w]hen they moved to
[Ch]icago.

Van Sicklen Speedmeters for Ford Cars

The Bracket Type

Where a Speedmeter alone is desired,
the Bracket Type gives a strictly high
grade instrument in every respect. It
can be depended upon for accuracy at
all times and the large, black-face dial
with its clean cut figures make its reading easy when running at any speed.

Price Complete $12.00

The George W. Ludlow Co., a major producer of shoes, moved from Chicago to Elgin in 1891, attracted by the offer of a new factory near the northeast corner of Congdon and Dundee avenues. Selz-Schwab bought the plant in 1897. This firm was producing up to 2,000 pairs of women's shoes daily before it closed in 1929.

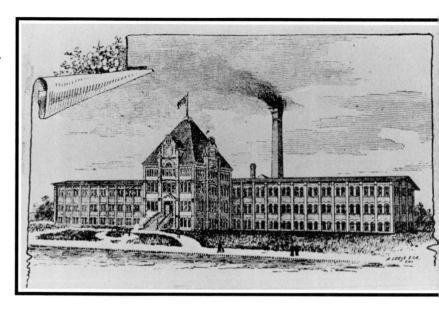

The former shoe factory later housed the B. G. Garment Co. (women's dresses), a neon sign maker, Brody, Inc. (women's coats), and Tiny Tim, a miniature golf course. The State of Illinois operated a district highway sign shop in the building. In 1940 it employed six painters and four outside construction men. The unit produced and maintained more than 21,000 signs for the 1,500 miles of state primary roads in eight northern Illinois counties.

The Elgin Stove & Oven Co. produced gas ranges in a plant on North State Street between 1923 and 1931. The firm began making steel kitchen cabinets, which became the chief product line, in 1927. Production ended in 1957.

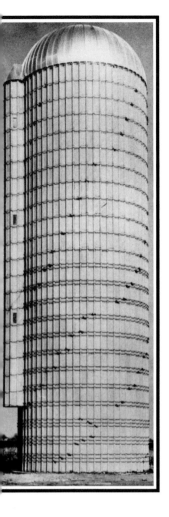

Founded as a partnership about 1914, the firm of Mason and Lawrence manufactured the Ribstone silo. The roofs and concrete staves were made at the plant on Ann Street; the steel reinforcement rods were purchased. In 1934 Mason and Lawrence built one of its largest silos for the Belvidere Canning Co. It was seventy feet in diameter, thirty feet high, and held 5,000 tons of silage.

David H. Butler in 1890 purchased a small factory making hard and soft soap for the local market. The business expanded with the introduction of powdered soap in 1897 and was incorporated as the Elgin National Soap Co. in 1906.

I Favor The Adoption
of Voting Machines
For Elgin

INTERNATIONAL

V O T I N G

MACHINE

Voting machines were a short-lived enterprise. Sales were slow, and the manufacturer pushed through a referendum calling for the city of Elgin to purchase them. Ten machines, each weighing about 400 pounds, were ordered in 1913 but never used, and the company folded after a court ruled that it was infringing upon a prior patent.

Rinehimer Bros. Mfg. Co., a family enterprise for nearly a century, developed from a small planing mill on River Street in 1867. Emmanuel Rinehimer was succeeded in the business by two sons, Charles E. Rinehimer and Albert C. Rinehimer, and a grandson, Charles A. Rinehimer. The plant pictured above was erected at the northwest corner North Grove Avenue and Kimball Street in 1910. It was leveled in 1966, the last property razed for the Civic Center development. The business changed hands that year and became Rinehimer Woodwork Corp.

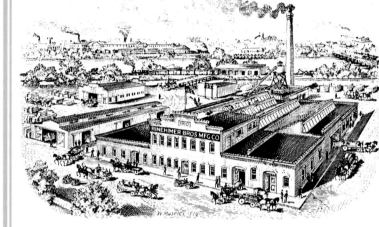

RINEHIMER BROS. MFG. CO.
Manufacturers of
SASH—DOORS—STAIRS—INTERIOR FINISH

Rinehimer employees are shown here as they appeared about 1910. In its early years the company's output consisted of sash, screens, doors, blinds, and mouldings, and later the firm specialized in architectural woodwork with a wide market in the Middle West. When St. John's Lutheran Church was erected in 1911-12, a Rinehimer employee worked 623 hours on its new pulpit.

Arthur Leath opened an upholstery repair shop in 1903. About 1907, when the business was incorporated, he began manufacturing three-piece parlor suites, later adding dining room chairs and mattresses. At first a mail order business, its output was later marketed through its own retail chain. When Leath died in 1927, the firm was operating thirty-two retail stores in five states. Furniture manufacturing in Elgin ceased in 1931 with the deepening Depression.

Clarence Strite invented an automatic pop-up toaster in 1919, but it was not widely available for home use until Max McGraw purchased the patent in 1926 and organized the McGraw Electric Co. to tap the mass market. Toastmaster production, which had been started in Minneapolis, was shifted to Elgin in 1938. The manufacturing facilities were relocated to Iowa in 1966, and in 1980 the corporate offices were removed to Rolling Meadows.

Pictured is a two-slice "Powermatic," 1080 watts, shipping weight 6-1/2 pounds, listed in the 1961 catalog.

An early Ford dealer, John M. Murphy was an alderman from the fourth ward when he was named the city's superintendent of streets. This position led to an interest in how to keep them clean. His solution was a motorized sweeper which would sprinkle the dust with water, collect the dirt and refuse, and dump them into a box.

Murphy's sweeper had three wheels—two in back and one in front for maneuverability—with a dirt box in front, engine in the rear and broom in between. His invention was financed and manufactured by the American Tower and Tank Co., now the Elgin Sweeper Co., which had been making structural steel for water towers and buildings in Elgin since 1903. The first sweeper was sold to Boise, Idaho, in 1914. More than 20,000 have been delivered to cities all over the world.

The broad range of Elgin's industrial output over the years has also included chewing gum, cotton batting, woven wire fencing, caramel candy, machinery for perforating piano rolls, radios, phonograph records, cigars, water softeners, corsets, packaging machinery, kerosene cans, and automobile spotlights.

Elgin's first schools were supported by private subscription; it wasn't until 1851 that local taxes were levied for education. The city government operated the schools, beginning in 1854, until a separate school district was organized in 1873.

Elgin High, one of the oldest continuously existing secondary schools in Illinois, was established in 1869 and held its first commencement three years later. The oldest parochial school is St. John's Lutheran, whose first classes were held in the church in 1866.

t all Elgin schools were brick. ese two were built from a similar sign about 1870. The "watch fac- y" school at what is now National d Villa streets, pictured right, was ved to the southwest corner of St. arles and Bent streets after the tional Street School was opened 1883. In its new location it was led the Bent Street School. Above the North or Brook Street School the northwest corner of Brook and erry streets. Both buildings were andoned in 1906.

Schools, like the children they serve, grow in size. The National Street School was erected in 1883, with two rooms finished and furnished. The building was completed as a four-room school the next year. A basement room was added in 1890, and a five room addition was made in 1891. The building was expanded again in 1898, when it was renamed Lincoln School. A new west wing contained the furnace room, and the old furnace room was converted into a classroom. A room fifteen-feet square was fitted up for storing student bicycles. Lincoln was vacated in 1968 when the new Channing Memorial School opened. It was razed in 1978, and its site was developed into a neighborhood park.

St. Mary's opened its doors as an academy for young ladies in February 1880. It is still standing on Villa Street near Fulton. The first diplomas were issued in 1883. One of the alumni was Anna Lynch, an internationally-known portrait and miniature painter and the first Elgin-born woman to be listed in Who's Who in America. When a new building was constructed in 1924-25, the old St. Mary's was occupied by the Turners.

eachers and upper-grade students are posed in front of the ew Brick School in 1882. At the left are Alfred S. Barry, rincipal, and Ida Clifford, teacher. Fourth girl from the ft in the second row is Hattie Pease, donator of the emmens Auditorium in the Civic Center.

A two-story and basement brick high school was erected on DuPage near Chapel, just east of the Old Brick, in 1883-84. Old Brick was removed after it was completed, giving the new building an expanse of lawn to the west as well as a park to the south. On a summer's night hundreds of swallows circled the tower for an hour or two and then disappeared into the two large chimneys.

Increasing enrollments led to an expansion of the high school (left) beginning in 1905-06. A third story was added to the east wing and the old building was raised in 1909-10. The west wing and center section were finished in 1911.

These views of a chemistry laboratory and an English classroom were taken about 1904.

Grant and McKinley schools, of similar design, both opened in 1886 and are still in use. Each school was a four-room brick building with high ceilings, steam heat and outdoor privies. Grant, originally called the Mill Street School, opened on September 7th and McKinley, the Prospect Street School, began classwork on September 13th. The tower, called the "cuckoo room," of McKinley, pictured above, was removed in 1911. Indoor toilets were installed in 1913.

This was the school that twice fulfilled the dreams and hopes of many students. The Locust Street School, occupying an entire block between Elm and Perry, was constructed in 1880 and completely destroyed by fire on January 21, 1884. One of the electric arc light towers erected in 1883 can be seen at the right. It was brought crashing to the ground by the Palm Sunday tornado of 1920.

Renamed, in 1905, in honor of the philanthropist, George P. Lord, the school on Locust Street went up in flames again on February 7, 1906. It was rebuilt and opened the following year. The school was closed for financial reasons in 1939. Catholic parishes bought the building, and it became St. Edward High School in 1941. After additions were made to this central core, it was torn down in 1967.

The unusually ornate Franklin School opened November 17, 1891. It had a balcony, basement play room, and dark green chalkboards. One of the first faculty members was May Davidson, a granddaughter of Elgin's founder, James T. Gifford. Because of overflow enrollment, high school classes occupied all or part of the building from 1899 to 1911. Franklin was closed after Channing Memorial School opened and is now occupied by the Community Crisis Center.

The new Elgin High School was dedicated June 8, 1911. It contained fifty rooms and had an enrollment capacity of 1,050. The library was located on the second floor over the main entrance. Above the auditorium, which seated 1,100, was a gymnasium with a running track and shower baths. The building was equipped with a private telephone system and pneumatic clocks.

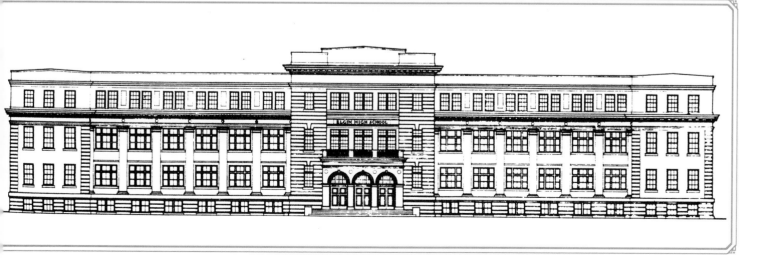

ALUMNI

Elgin classrooms have educated men and women of achievement in many fields. In addition to the five pictured here, they included presidents of Encyclopedia Britannica, Republic Steel, and Greyhound (now the Dial Corporation); an authority on the economy of the Soviet Union; a commander of the Naval Air Force, U. S. Atlantic Fleet; and a Pulitzer Prize winning TV critic.

Son of a Fountain Square clothing merchant, Max Adler of Elgin High's Class of 1883 became a violin virtuoso after his studies at Berlin's Royal Conservatory and played in concert halls here and abroad. He later was associated with Sears, Roebuck and Co., retiring as vice president and general manager in 1928, and donated the Adler Planetarium to the city of Chicago.

Inventor, newsman, social reformer and novelist, Frederick U. Adams was graduated from Elgin High School in 1876. His monograph, "Atmospheric Resistance and Its Relation to the Speed of Railway Trains," published in 1893, led to America's first experimental streamliner. A novel, *John Burt*, was a best seller in 1902. Adams' electric lamppost, patented in 1889, became the model generally adopted.

Gail M. Dack, Elgin High School Class of '18, was a pioneer in food poisoning research. A faculty member of the University of Chicago, 1925-1966, he was director of its Food Research Institute which studied staphylococal food poisoning and botulism. His textbook, *Food Poisoning*, went through three editions.

President, chief executive officer and chairman of the Board of General Motors Corporation, 1965-1971, James M. Roche was the first graduate of Elgin High School to appear on the cover of Time magazine. Roche, a member of the Class of '23, didn't attend college. He joined GM in 1927 as a statistician in a Cadillac sales and service branch in Chicago.

Paul J. Flory, Elgin High School Class of '27, became one of the leading researchers in the chemistry of macromolecules and polymers after receiving his doctorate from Ohio State University. He was awarded a Nobel Prize in 1974 for "fundamental achievements, both theoretical and experimental," in the field of physical chemistry, which includes synthetic fibers, plastics and biological compounds. A professor at Stanford University, he became a spokesman for activist groups trying to protect Soviet scientists.

Tom Shales, Elgin High School Class of '62, became television editor for the Washington *Post* in 1977. His column, "On the Air," is nationally syndicated. "He has been called brilliant, thoughtful, incisive and screamingly funny," reported *Time* magazine, June 8, 1981. "Also vicious, infuriating, cruel and unfair." Shales received the Pulitzer Prize for criticism in 1988.

CHURCHES

The religious feelings which have deeply influenced the lives of Elgin residents can't be visualized as easily as the buildings reared for their worship services. Churches have interesting histories. A few of them are related here.

Built in 1866-1867 for a pioneer merchant, William G. Hubbard, this eleven-room home was purchased in 1873 by Gail Borden, inventor of a process for canning milk. Borden died January 11, 1874, before occupying the property. His widow, Emeline lived here until her death in 1890. The house was remodeled twice by the Christian Scientists for use as a church, 1919-1957, and it was later occupied by the First Christian Church, 1957-1967, and the Calvary Baptist Church, 1967-1972.

e arrival of the watch factory brought a
sh influx of New Englanders, including
ongregationalists and Universalists, to
gin. Many of the foremen and skilled work-
en were natives of Massachusetts. The
iversalists erected this building in 1866-67
the southeast corner of DuPage and Villa
reets. By 1891 it had become too small for
e membership and needed repairs. Two of
e pinnacles had fallen off, and others were
longer perpendicular. The church was
oved to an adjacent lot to the east and
modeled as Unity Hall, a place for banquets
d social events. Although extensively
modeled in 1908, when brick siding was
ded, it is probably the oldest surviving
ructure in the downtown area.

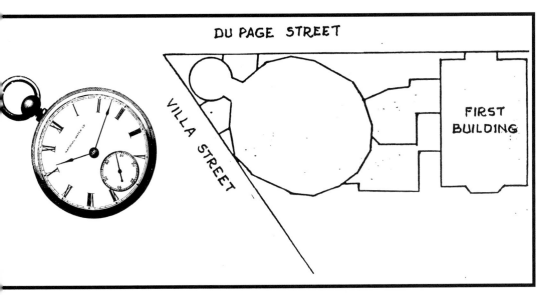

When looked at from above,
the former First Universalist
Church is in the shape of a
pocket watch. A round
vestibule represents the stem
winder ring. The sixteen-sided
auditorium is the face or dial.

1892 the Universalists completed a new
uilding well adapted to the triangular shape
the site. Plans were drawn under the leader-
ip of George Hunter, then superintendent of
e Elgin National Watch Co. The pews were
rranged in amphitheater style, and the audi-
rium was often used for lectures by promi-
nt visitors, such as Lincoln Steffens and
orman Thomas. A bomb blew out eight win-
ows in the church, known for the liberal views
its members, in 1970. The building was rav-
ged by a fire in 1977. It was placed on the
ational Register of Historic Places in 1980.

National offices of the Church of the Brethren are located in Elgin. When they arrived in 1899, members wore somber clothes, the women in black bonnets, and the men in black hats with wide brims. The Brethren practiced foot washing, following the example of Jesus, in John 13:4-5, who "rose from supper, laid aside his garments, and girded himself with a towel. Then he poured water into a basin, and began to wash the disciples' feet, and to wipe them with the towel with which he was girded."

Both the First Baptist and the Second Baptist churches once baptized members in the Fox River, regardless of the temperature.

The Presbyterians dedicated this fine new church on the southwest corner of Chicago and Center streets on July 11, 1872. It was destroyed by fire the following December 5th. The congregation, without a building and burdened with debt, managed to dedicate a new church on the site in December 1873.

The replacement, now one of the oldest structures in downtown Elgin, served the Presbyterians until it was sold to the newly-organized St. Joseph Catholic Church in 1887. This parish soon outgrew the little chapel and moved to Division Street in 1903. The building later became the Masonic Temple and then a hall for the Knights of Columbus.

In some mass-produced housing projects, a small house can be erected on a slab in less than thirty days. But to complete, inside and out, a church seating 250 people with an eight-foot basement and a tower fifty-feet high in 26-1/2 working days from groundbreaking to final decoration? The feat was accomplished for the Cedar Hill Mission by an avid congregation of the First Evangelical Church (now Faith United Methodist) and a small army of construction workers unemployed after the Panic of '93. It was subsequently used, for about forty years, by what is now the First Assembly of God. The building, its appearance much altered, is still standing at Crystal and Silver streets.

The original Center Building, under construction during the years 1870-1874, is still standing, although it has not been occupied by patients since 1973. The huge, pink-roofed, silver-domed structure is more than 1,000 feet in length. In order to secure the hospital, the City of Elgin donated the 155-acre Chisholm farm, the use of a spring, and free freight over the Chicago & North Western railroad.

In 1886 an irregularly-shaped artificial lake, 400 by 150 feet in area, was formed as a storage reservoir. It was spanned by a rustic bridge and dotted with several islets.

8

The site of a state mental hospital and two general hospitals—Sherman and St. Joseph—Elgin has become a major medical center providing professional services for a wide area encompassing parts of three counties.

The first patients entered the Northern Illinois Hospital and Asylum for the Insane, now the Elgin Mental Health Center, in 1872. In the early years care was largely custodial. Patients were isolated and locked in their rooms at night. Later they were "kept busy" working on the hospital's farm, grounds, kitchens and laundry.

With the erection of the Annex Building in 1891, the asylum's capacity was increased by 300 patients. Dining rooms were in the center section; the wings were dormitories. The new unit filled quickly, and by June of that year the patient census reached 1,010. The Annex housed patients until 1960. It was razed in the summer of 1972.

Erected in 1921-22, this was the first Illinois state building to be devoted exclusively to the care of mental cases among veterans of the World War. Its capacity was 225. The needs of returning servicemen was one of the reasons the patient census rose to 2,571 in 1923.

Henry Sherman, a pioneer who arrived in 1838, was one of the original stockholders in the watch company. In 1888, learning that the newly organized Woman's Club was interested in establishing a hospital, he donated a two-story house and lot on the northeast corner of Channing and North streets.

The first Sherman Hospital building on Channing Street was ready on July 7, 1888. There were only four patient rooms, but they were "open to the sick of all classes without regard to religion, nationality, sex or color." Of the thirty-six patients admitted the first year, twelve were discharged as "cured" and eighteen were "improved." One of the first admissions was a small black cat with a broken paw who stayed on as the official mouser and later became an obstetrical case.

A larger Sherman Hospital on Center Street was ready for occupancy in November 1895. There were seventeen patient rooms, two operating rooms, sleeping rooms for nurses, and an apartment for the superintendent. Down through 1930 the hospital was managed and financed by the Woman's Club.

erman Hospital was founded at
ime when new procedures were
ginning to make hospitals safer.
e idea of antisepsis was more or
ss accepted, and anesthesia
ade possible more extended and
licate operations. This is a
rgery scene in the nineties.

e hospital was extended along Center Street northward
the corner of Cooper by additions completed in 1917 and
27. Total bed capacity rose to 135.

The Franciscan Sisters of the Sacred Heart opened St. Joseph Hospital in a converted frame residence at Prospect Street and Jefferson Avenue on February 24, 1902. During the first year 125 patients were admitted, one fifth of them charity cases.

A new brick building containing twenty-five beds was erected in 1904 at the southwest corner of Prospect and Jefferson.

The building was expanded to conta[in] sixty beds in 1914, and in 1926 a fou[r] story addition increased capacity to 150 beds and thirty bassinets. The last enlargement included a chapel. St. Joseph Hospital sponsored a Nurses' Training School, 1919 to 1948.

A new hospital was completed on a thirty-three-acre site on the west si[de] in 1973. The former location—the block bounded by Jefferson and Plum, Prospect and Center—was donated to the City of Elgin and wa[s] developed into St. Francis Park in 1974.

Although many fine old homes and buildings have vanished over the years, Elgin has a greater architectural diversity than most communities. In addition to a variety of nineteenth century styles, there are differences in size and construction materials. Mail order houses, brick flats, Victorian ladies —painted and plain—four-squares, cobblestones, former boardinghouses, converted stores, and concrete block bungalows are the reasons the city remains unique amid the suburban sprawl.

the absence of architects in Elgin's early years, builders sed design books from which the prospective owners could ake selections. David Whitney Bangs recalled that he uilt the house of sement (sic) that Tuck lives in 1850 and nished it in 1852." The house is still standing at 118 ennyson Court. A twin was constructed about the same me on the north side of what is now Big Timber Road. The riginal design was Greek Revival.

illiam C. Kimball erected this two-ory brick hill top mansion in 1870, e year before he was elected mayor of lgin. Set on two and a half acres of ound, the house represented an origi-al investment of $25,000, an enormous m in a day when most men had an nnual income of less than $500. The ouse contained 18 rooms finished in ack walnut and cherry. The house is ill standing, although the veranda as been removed.

Brick Flats

One of the finer homes of early Elgin was "Grand View," a solid brick, eleven-room mansion erected for Andrew Jackson Waldron in the fifties. When first built, the home was considered to be in the country. The cupola on the roof provided a "grand view" of the surrounding area from its hilltop site on South Gifford Street. The home was razed in 1976.

Waldron, an early justice of the peace, township supervisor and mayor, was a banker, attorney, and insurance and real estate agent. He was one of the organizers of the Fox River Valley Railroad, later known as the east side or "low" North Western.

Many American eight-sided buildings were inspired by Orson Squire Fowler's book, *A Home for All*, first published in 1848. The author claimed they increased airflow and made possible well-lit interiors. Elgin's "Old Octagon," on the southwest corner of Chapel and Fulton streets, was erected in the fifties and became a rooming house for watch workers. It was badly damaged by fire in 1897 and torn down.

orkers pouring into a booming Elgin in the late eighties
nd early nineties required rental housing until they
uld afford homes of their own. This need was met by
rick flats, many of them designed and built by Gilbert
. Turnbull. The lower floor was partly below ground
vel, and the steps of the ornamented wooden porch led
 the second floor entrance. They usually had overhang-
g metal cornices and rectangular bays. Stained glass
lged the front windows, and red brick trim provided dec-
ation.

Elegant interiors once adorned large Elgin homes built in the late nineteenth century. Ornate oak trim and stained glass greeted visitors in the entry of a home erected in 1893 for Charles V. McClure, a lumber dealer. The winding stairway has hand-carved spindles.

Intricate carvings flank one of the fireplaces in the McClure home. The mantles, buffet and a china cabinet were the work of a German woodcarver.

The Delmont E. Wood home, which once stood at 170 South State Street, was built in 1884. Wood was one of the leading creamery operators. An ornate stairway was lighted by a stained glass window, and elaborate tiles decorated a fireplace.

Despite the efforts of Paul Durrenberger, who drew the exterior view pictured, to preserve this home, it was torn down for a parking lot in 1980.

"Peace," a home that once stood on South State Street, was erected for Joshua Palmer Morgan in 1849. It was designed in the Greek Revival style, but a cupola was added and the original Corinthian columns were replaced by bracketed supports. The home was later purchased by the owner of a gold and silver mine in Utah and then by a proprietor of Wizard Oil, a widely advertised patent medicine. Converted into an apartment house, with columns restored, it was razed in 1969 for a high rise.

Not all interior decoration had to be costly. This Douglas avenue home utilized an ivy plant to give a room a natural look.

M. C. Eppenstein was the chief owner and organizer of the Illinois Watch Case Co. His mansion at 230 South State Street was erected in the late nineties. Third floor windows overlooked a broad spectrum of the east side of the city. After Eppenstein's death in 1921 the home was converted into nine apartments. It was damaged in a fire on November 27, 1960 and demolished the following year for a luxury apartment building.

The "high North
Western" station, the
American House—an
early hotel—and
dwellings can be seen in
this view of the west
side in the sixties. And
what are those narrow
structures along the
river bank?

So many householders cared for chickens as well as children in their back yards that a local poultry show was held annually beginning in 1900. Stores advertised incubators, wire, feed, scratch and mash. Chicken coops were almost as common as that ever-present necessity shown at the right.

he Board of Education in 1895 defended a decision incorporate inside closets at Washington School listing some of the objectionable features of out-de privies, even when they were as well made as e one at the left. "They are an eyesore to all; it is npossible to keep them free from the most foul dors...in winter, cold and unhealthy; cannot be kept cked, as the locks are broken; depravations of all inds are committed; obscene writings and figures n the walls; a receptacle for tramps...."

ne of the last of the city's outhouses was tipped ver by Halloween pranksters in 1936. It was a two-eater decorated with the customary half-moon and tar-shaped vents.

OperaHouse ELGIN ILLS.

FRED W. JENCKS, Manager

BILL O' THE PLAY

Vol. 1.   Thursday, December 25, 1903.   No. 28.

"THE BURGLAR"

Traveling stock companies, featuring some of the leading figures of the American theater—E. H. Sothern, Julia Marlowe, Minnie Maddern Fiske, Edwin Booth, and Otis Skinner—presented melodramas at the Opera House. More than plays occupied the stage. There were minstrel shows and marathon walkers, politicians and evangelists, and now and then even an opera. About the time the Opera House was remodeled into the Grand Theater in 1910, vaudeville was replacing the road shows. The Marx Brothers played here, and so did Al Jolson.

Card playing, enjoyed by this Elgin foursome about 1898, was a common form of recreation but was often proscribed by clergymen. Billy Sunday, the evangelist, came to Elgin for a big revival in 1900 and declaimed: "Our vows to God are soon forgotten in the dance hall, at the card party and other questionable places."

SPORTS & RECREATION

10

When the work week at the watch factory was six ten-hour days, and Sunday was considered a day of rest, there wasn't much time for recreation. Reading, sleigh rides and ice skating, fishing, occasional dances, and performances at the Opera House were some of the uses of the limited leisure time. Then, in the nineties, came the big new parks, cycling, and the beginning of high school sports.

...fter the "safety," with ...oth wheels the same size, ...d the pneumatic tire ...ere introduced, the popu-...rity of the bicycle ...came widespread. By ...391 cyclists were doing ...e "century"—a hundred ...iles in one day—on a tri-...gular route from Elgin ... Chicago and back by ...ay of Naperville and ...urora. Riding clubs ...ganized races and tours. ...hese young sports and ...eir wheels are sitting in ...ifford Park. The old ...igh school building is in ...e background.

Back in 1875, before there was a National or an American League, when baseball was played without gloves, the amateur Bluff Citys claimed the state championship. The local Advocate was pleased to report that the club "has received many complimentary notices in different newspapers for the gentlemanly conduct of its members."

Elgin had teams in two ill-fated minor league franchises in professional baseball. In 1910 the local Kittens were the leading team when the Northern Association folded. In 1915 the Pirates, photo right, were in third place with a won-lost record of 23-23 when the Bi-State League collapsed.

The Marguerite Block, fronting on East Chicago Street at the river's edge, was completed for the David C. Cook Publishing Co. in 1889. The YMCA, reorganized in 1882, occupied the ground floor of this building in 1895. When Cook's moved to a new plant in the north end in 1901, the Y took over all the firm's former plant. The Association remained in this location until 1956.

The YMCA's Boys' Department organized graded gym classes, games, outing and a camping program. Here is a young gymnastics team in 1907 with the regulation gray knee pants and black stockings. Sunday afternoon speakers, many of them clergymen, described the evils of cigarettes and liquor and provided moral lessons.

Two teachers, Hattie Griffin and Myrtle Huff, who were concerned about the lack of recreation for the large number of working women in Elgin, were the moving spirits behind the formation of the YWCA in 1901. The first social and physical activities were scheduled in the watch factory gymnasium. The Y's first building, opened in 1906, featured a cafeteria. A swimming pool was added in 1913. The Whitford apartments, shown at the right of the photograph were acquired in 1918 for resident members. The present building was erected in stages, 1965-1966.

Elgin High's first interscholastic football game resulted in a 5 to 0 win over an Elgin Academy eleven on October 23, 1891. The school lost its first interscholastic basketball game, played March 2, 1900, to Englewood, 16 to 12. These were the basketball and football uniforms of the Maroons in 1911-1912.

"Some of the girls have organized a basket ball team," reported the *Elgin Daily News*, September 21, 1901. "Everything has been planned, even to the suits which are going to be dreams—or more truly nightmares." This team played girls from other schools, beating the big Rockford High contingent twice. In 1907 the Illinois High School Athletic Association prohibited girls interscholastic basketball, giving as one reason "the exercise in public is immodest and not altogether lady-like."

In 1924 and 1925 Elgin High School was the first team to win the state basketball championship two years in succession. The '24 Maroons, shown here, were undefeated in their conference and eliminated eight opponents in tournament play before downing Athens in the final. Reports of the big game were relayed from Urbana to Villa Olivia for broadcasting by Charley Erbstein's radio station WTAS.

Coach John Krafft's Maroons were among the Sweet Sixteen in 1943, 1944 and 1945, compiling sixty wins against only thirteen losses in the three seasons. The 1943 Krafft Kids, pictured left, were the Big Eight champions.

Earl T. (Tanner) Britton was one of Elgin's greatest athletes. A fullback at Elgin High, he scored seven touchdowns in one game in 1921 and finished the season with 157 points, a school record. A blocking back for Red Grange at the University of Illinois, he preserved an undefeated season in 1923 with a fifty-five-yard field goal. His coach, Bob Zuppke, called him "one of the greatest punters and place kickers of all time." Britton played professionally in the National Football League, 1925-1929.

Beginning in 1923 Elgin hosted a number of ice skating meets in Lords Park, and local racers often traveled to other cities. The big Tri-State competition was an annual event from 1938 through 1942 and 1946-1954, except for 1950, when an unusually mild winter forced cancellation. Above is a scene from 1940.

An amusement park opened at Trout Park in the north end of the city on May 29, 1909. The biggest attraction was a "circle dip" roller coaster, the first of its kind. Among the other rides were a circle swing, a carousel, and ocean wave, steel boats and a miniature railway. The park ran full swing for a fortnight and then died by degrees. By the end of the season the owners were showered with levies, judgments and writs of attachment.

The first local movie house, a five-center or nickelodeon, opened in a converted grocery store on Grove Avenue in 1907. After the Grand Theater was destroyed in the Palm Sunday tornado, it was rebuilt as the Rialto and opened in 1921. The seating capacity was about 1,350, and the entrance under the marquee was separate from the exit. In 1928 the Rialto was the first Elgin theater to show a "talkie." The building was destroyed by fire in December 1956.

Although locally-devised telephones were put into service not long after Bell's invention was announced, the city's first exchange wasn't ready until 1881. Pictured here is a new telephone pole being erected outside the Hubbard Block in 1898.

In 1888 water began flowing in city mains from this pumping station located in the northeast end of the city. The water, drawn from the middle of the river, was piped into a reservoir, put through six filters, and then pumped into the standpipe. This tower, some 200 feet above the level of the river, held 525,000 gallons, and gravity pressure could throw water to a height of 100 feet downtown. The increasingly polluted Fox and periodic dry spells led to the use of artesian wells beginning in 1904.

Urban populations, especially as density per square mile increases, require governmental services. The city government was called upon to preserve the peace, fight fires, regulate public utilities and the sale of liquor, maintain streets and sewers, provide a water supply, and establish parks for recreation.

or more than forty years, Elgin's gas upply was manufactured from coal in plant along the west bank of the ver. Located between what are now e North Western and Soo Line acks north of the end of Standish treet, construction began in 1871. he original structures consisted of a tort building, where the gas was enerated by heating the coal in the osence of air, and a gas holder.

he local firm was merged into the estern United Gas & Electric Co. in)05, which achieved economies of ale by erecting a huge Koppers yproduct coke oven plant near Joliet 1912. Gas was pumped to Elgin rough an eight-inch main, and the is works was shut down in 1915.

The gas storage tank along St. Charles Street, erected in 1913, was 156 feet in diameter. Throughout the day as gas was used, the lifts dropped lower and lower until they were all in one container unit at the bottom. Underground gas storage and new pipelines curtailed its usefulness, and it was dismantled in 1959.

Elgin's first patrol wagon made its trial run in May 1891. It wasn't used much until the city council got around to appropriating money to maintain a team of horses at a livery stable.

In 1896 the police force comprised a marshal, three sergeants, a jailer, the patrol wagon driver, four night patrolmen, two day patrolmen, and a half-day man. Most of the arrests were for drunken and disorderly conduct, which kept the patrol wagon busy. It made 456 runs that year.

A later model was introduced in 1908. When the Ford police wagon-ambulance arrived in 1915, the first passenger was a ten-year old boy who had wandered from home.

lgin's fourth City Hall was built on the site of a former aymarket on the northeast corner of Chicago and Spring treets. It was first occupied on July 17, 1893. Of ictorian-Gothic design, its red-brick exterior was topped by clock tower and peaked slate roof. Mayor William Grote onated the town clock. The three floors and basement ere too large for the city's needs at the time, and the third oor was left unfinished.

he Palm Sunday tornado of 1920 knocked the building out f line. The damage was patched up, but the structure was eakened, and it wasn't considered safe to complete the ird floor.

oliticians and city employees were not the only inhabitants f the old City Hall. In 1925 it was infested by rats, and ttempts were made to eliminate them with poisoned fish nd hamburger. The results were disappointing. In ctober of that year the *Daily Courier* reported that a large at became hopelessly intoxicated on whiskey and wine ash seized in a Prohibition raid.

ARWIN E. PRICE

PEOPLES

CANDIDATE FOR MAYOR

ELECTION APRIL 16, 1907

The increased role of government in the lives of Elgin residents enlivened city politics. One of the leading actors in the local dramatic productions at City Hall was Arwin E. Price, a clarion-voiced marble cutter who served six terms as mayor from 1889 through 1927. A magnetic tribune of the people, Price was loved by many, a large portion of whom were champions of the freedom to imbibe, and detested by others, particularly church women.

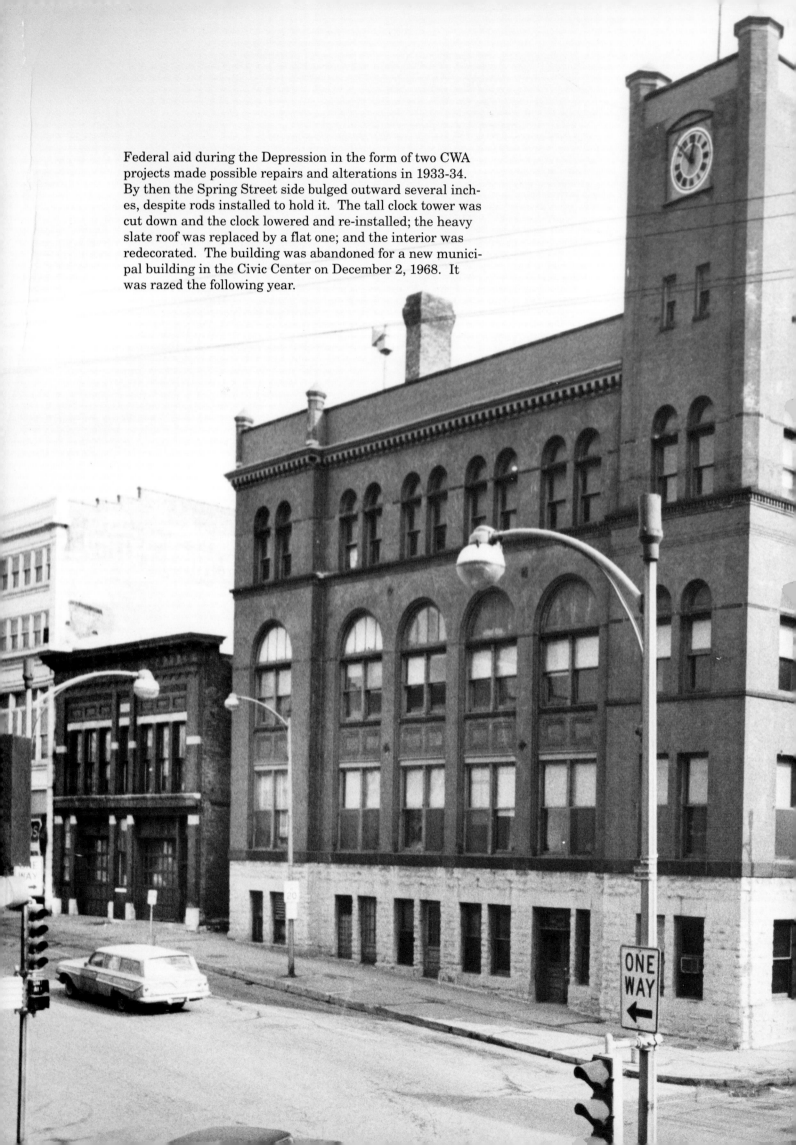

Federal aid during the Depression in the form of two CWA projects made possible repairs and alterations in 1933-34. By then the Spring Street side bulged outward several inches, despite rods installed to hold it. The tall clock tower was cut down and the clock lowered and re-installed; the heavy slate roof was replaced by a flat one; and the interior was redecorated. The building was abandoned for a new municipal building in the Civic Center on December 2, 1968. It was razed the following year.

Volunteer firefighters are ranged along an upraised wooden sidewalk on Grove Avenue in this photograph taken in the early seventies. At the left is the combined City Hall and engine house completed in 1869-70. The tower was used to locate fires because there were no alarm boxes or telephones. In front of the building is the "James T. Gifford" steam fire engine purchased in 1869. It was a Silsby model with a 600-gallon pumping capacity. The two-wheeled hose carts carried 1500 feet of rubber hose. At the extreme right is the DuBois Opera House.

The former Fire Station No. 1, adjacent to the city hall on North Spring Street, opened in 1889. It was abandoned in 1968 when a new station opened in the municipal building in the Civic Center. All the early stations were known as "fire barns" because the equipment was horse-drawn.

Fire Station No. 5, located in a triangle formed by St. Charles Street and Arlington Avenue, was opened in January 1904. It was the last horse barn. Bales of hay were dropped through a trap door from the third floor down to the first floor stables. The station had lead-lined window panes.

Fire Station No. 4 at 36 Dubois Avenue served as a recreation center for neighborhood children. It was completed in 1896 but not occupied by a fire company until August 1, 1897. The station was vacated, 1932-1939, as an economy measure during the Depression. During the interim, the Good Shepherd Lutheran Church held its first worship service here on November 20, 1938.

The building was replaced by a new station on Larkin Avenue in 1968. Used for a time as a classroom to alleviate crowded conditions at Abbott School, it was converted into a residence in 1977. The traditional brass fire pole was retained.

Elgin's first motorized fire truck, a Packard, arrived in February 1916. It was equipped with hose, a chemical tank, and two extension ladders. The truck had solid rubber tires, a four-cylinder engine, and a maximum speed of tirty-five miles per hour. The manufacturer sent an instructor to teach the firefighters how to drive the apparatus, and the chief said every member of the fire department had to learn to drive. The last horse-drawn response to a fire alarm occurred on June 28, 1922.

The Packard is shown here as it appeared in 1919 in front of Station No. 2 on West Chicago Street.

On July 8, 1865 a fire swept the north side of Main (now East Chicago) Street from the "low" North Western tracks west to within a short distance of Market (now Fountain) Square. Among the businesses destroyed was R. W. Padelford's daguerrean gallery. Since he was also the city clerk, all municipal records went up in flames. Another fire, probably of incendiary origin, broke out on the Square in October of that year, prompting the City Council to offer a reward for the arrest of the perpetrator.

The fires stimulated an interest in fire protection. An alarm bell was placed in the tower of the woolen mill in 1867; volunteer fire companies were organized in 1868 and in 1869, the city purchased its first steam fire engine.

Two three-story tenements at 50 and 54 Walnut Avenue were destroyed by fire in April 1911, leaving thirty people homeless. Most of the occupants' personal effects were wiped out. Neighbors placed their available rooms at the disposal of the victims.

The Woodruff & Edwards foundry fire in November 1917 could be seen from every part of the city. Embers flew high in the air as the flames roared and crackled. Only the moulding room at the extreme north end of the property and a portion of the storeroom remained. Thousands of finished castings of school desks, the chief product of the company, and many coffee mills were part of the debris.

he Rialto Theater was destroyed by a spectacular fire on ecember 12, 1956. Two firefighters were working on the of when flames broke through, and parts of the roof gave ay. They made their way to a wall only to discover that it was beginning to collapse. They escaped, with leg injuries, by leaping across a four-foot gap to the roof of an adjacent building ten feet below.

George P. Lord was a business manager for the Elgin National Watch Co. and an investor in dairy farms. He served as a mayor of Elgin and a president of the board of education. Seventy years old and a widower, he married Mary Edwards Carpenter, an affluent widow in 1889. Childless and devoutly religious, they believed their wealth should be used to enrich the lives of their fellow citizens. Lords Park, Sherman Hospital, the YMCA, the Academy, and Oak Crest Residence were among the Elgin institutions benefiting from their philanthropies.

Once a farm owned by Dr. Joseph Tefft and later called Oakwood Park, George P. Lord purchased the property and deeded it to the city in 1893. Named Lords Park, it was expanded by subsequent additions.

"The park is designed for a public resting place," Lord stated in 1898. "From this standpoint who can estimate its value, or have any just conception of the benefits that may be derived from frequent and prolonged visits to its cool and refreshing retreats?"

By the end of the century Lords Park had been improved by two lagoons—formed by damming up Willow Creek—a pavilion, a bear cage, picturesque driveways, an enclosed woods for deer, and an electrically-lighted bandstand.

The first two black bears for the zoo, ...ck and Juno, arrived in 1896 and were ...ter joined by Frank and Kitty. Davey ...alker, park custodian, trained them to ...tricks, such as standing on their hind ...gs and kissing Davey on the cheek. ...he bear cage was filled and graded to ...e level of Willow Creek in 1969.

...he first park pavilion burned to the ground on September ...0, 1897 and was replaced by this larger, 2600-square-foot ...uilding the following year. Originally it housed Lord's col-...ction of mounted animals and oil paintings.

Construction of the Neo-Classic natural history museum in Lords Park began in 1906. The central hall was completed that year, and the west wing was added in 1907. Interest declined after the death of George P. Lord, and the projected east and north wings were never built. The building was used for park storage and a dog pound until it finally opened in 1920 under the auspices of the Elgin Audubon Society. The city Parks and Recreation Department took over operation after the Society disbanded in 1961. Since 1983 it has been managed by the Elgin Public Museum, Inc.

A shelter house was located at the Forest Avenue entrance to the park opposite a terminus of the streetcar line.

160

William H. Wing—an attorney, bank director, and owner of farm land inherited from parents who arrived in Elgin in 1846—bequeathed the city 110 acres for the west side park which bears his name.

There were two springs in Wing Park. This was the iron or sulphur spring, so called because of the water's color.

Elgin's first bathing beach opened in Wing Park in 1907, the same year the Gentleman's Driving Club held its initial trotting races on a half-mile track. A nine-hole golf course was ready for play late in 1908.

The Elgin National Watch Co. contributed a huge sterling silver trophy to the winner of the main race, the Elgin National. It is 44 inches high and weighs 41 pounds. The winners, the names of the cars they drove, and their times are engraved on the trophy. The winner of the trophy was required to post a $5,000 bond to insure its return for the following year's race.

The eight and one-half mile long course allowed the cars to attain high average speeds. There were no steep hills, no railroad crossings, and no intersections. The road was graded and widened for the races, and oil was spread by horse-drawn equipment to settle the dust.

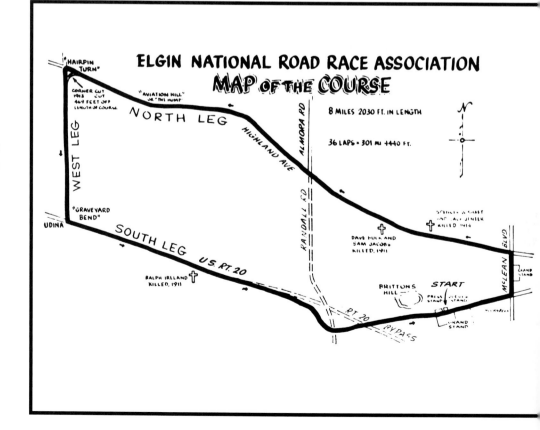

ROAD RACES

On a gravel and dirt track west of the city, men and machines competed in tests of speed and endurance known as the Elgin Road Races. Originally sponsored by the Chicago Motor Club and financed by a local corporation, the races were held in late August.

The main event, the Elgin National, was 305 miles in length in 1910, 1911 and 1912. It was reduced to 301 miles in 1913, 1914, 1915 and 1919 after "Hairpin Turn" in the northwest corner was cut down to reduce the possibilities of accidents and to increase speeds. The 1920 race was shortened to 30 laps or 250 miles. There were no races in 1916, 1917, and 1918 because of wartime restrictions, and after 1920 high speeds endangered spectators and forced their discontinuance.

Ralph Mulford, winner of the first Elgin National in 1910, drove the entire 36 laps with only one pit stop for gas, oil and water. This is how he recalled his experiences in Elgin: "I never competed in a race where better sportsmanship was displayed than in the Elgin National. Every driver was more than willing to give a faster car the right of way and often risked their lives by giving way in order to leave a clear track."

Farmers complained about closing the roads for practices and races and the disruption of their work. Their consent was necessary because spectators had to be kept behind fence lines. They were compensated by outright payments and shares in the receipts.

A mechanic rode in each car. He watched the gasoline and oil gauges, handled the jack if tire changes were necessary, and warned the driver of cars approaching from the rear. As the race wore on, dust rose in clouds, and the roadway—especially at the corners—became deeply rutted.

The Road Races attracted thousands of spectators and most local businesses closed on race days. The city took on a festive air. Shown here are the crowds on Fountain Square heading out to the track in 1910. (photo courtesy Chicago Historical Society)

163

Harry Grant in an Alco (No. 1) and Len Zengel driving a National (No. 2) were the first cars to start in the 1911 Elgin National. Zengel was the winner that year. (photo courtesy Chicago Historical Society)

All told, Ralph DePalma was the most successful driver at Elgin, winning six races. Three of his victories were in the Elgin National. He is pictured above in his Mercedes in 1912 and below in his Mercedes in downtown Elgin in 1914. In 1920 he won with a French-made Ballot.

Tires needed frequent changing. This was a scene in the pits in 1911. (photo courtesy Chicago Historical Society)

ddie Hearne is at the wheel of a chain-driven Fiat in this 1912 ace. The National Guard kept spectators away from the track.

In addition to the large scoreboard opposite the grandstand, there were smaller score boards placed around the course at intervals of one mile. Since the cars were started thirty seconds apart and the differences in times were not adjusted until the end of the race, it was difficult for most spectators to determine who was leading.

Around the course were dozens of spots where parties of motorists could spend the day amid rural scenes and smells watching the cars flash by or see them coming up long stretches of the road. In 1913 the spectators' cars had to be in their reserved parking places by 10:30 a.m. A series of aerial bombs gave warning when the course was completely closed to all traffic. No one was allowed to stand on or cross the road during the races and until twenty minutes after the last car had passed.

ELGIN AUTOMOBILE ROAD RACES

FRIDAY AND SATURDAY

AUGUST 29th, - 30th,

1913

ELGIN, ILLINOIS

COVERED GRAND STAND·

TICKETS ON SALE JUNE 15, 1913

ELGIN AUTOMOBILE ROAD RACE ASSN.

CHICAGO AUTOMOBILE CLUB

The races were advertised widely in periodicals, posters, and postcards.

In the early years there were two days of racing. The events on Friday were for cars with smaller engines than the big cars entered in the Elgin National on Saturday. After World War I, when the races were revived in 1919 and 1920, there was only one event, the Elgin National.

The driver of this Duesenberg in 1914 went seven laps in the Elgin National before retiring with a cracked cylinder. He was Eddie Rickenbacker, who became America's flying ace in World War I, downing sixteen German planes.

Spectators in the grandstand on Larkin Avenue await the start of an early race. Flagmen, usually on motorcycles, were stationed about the course for crowd control and to warn drivers of conditions beyond a curve or over a hill. A red flag was used to indicate the road ahead was clear. An obstruction was signalled by a yellow flag. A white flag informed the driver he must stop for consultation the next time he passed the judge's stand. A green flag stood for one more lap to go and the checkered flag saluted the winner.

Barney Oldfield, the famed driver, was never successful at Elgin. He is shown at the wheel of a Knox outside a Hoornbeek barn prior to the 1910 race.

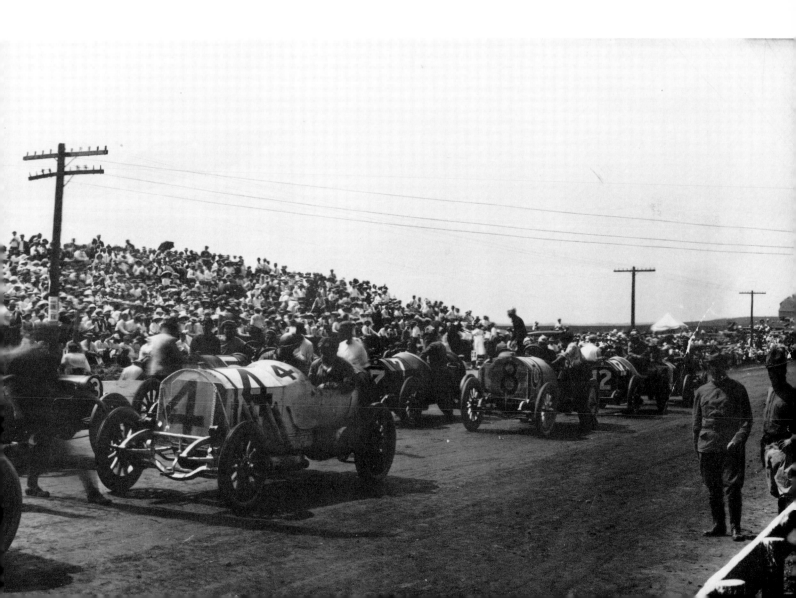

Competing cars were entered by various domestic and foreign manufacturers who hoped to use their makes' performances in company advertisements. The first cars were ordinary passenger vehicles, stripped for racing, with wooden wheels. In 1913 wire wheels made their appearance. By 1919 the machines had streamlined bodies and pointed tails, and the next year almost all the entries were fitted with four-wheel brakes.

There were many accidents, some of them fatal. In 1911 the main grandstand collapsed, injuring dozens; one driver was killed in a practice session; and a driver and his mechanic in Car No. 19, below, met death in the 1914 main event.

Car No. 2, a Mercedes, was out in front in the sixth lap in 1912 when this accident (top and left photos) occurred. The driver of Car No. 11 walked away unscathed.

Cars often "aviated" at a rise on the north leg. This rare photograph shows a DePalma-driven car with all four wheels of the track.

The road races were revived on August 26, 1933. Two 203-mile events were on the program, one for fourteen stock cars, mainly Fords, and one for special racing machines. Among the drivers were future Indy champions Wilbur Shaw and Mauri Rose. Some of the racers roared past the grandstand at speeds close to 115 miles per hour, and there was little protection for spectators who crowded around the course.

Phil (Red) Shafer (photo right) won the main event in a Buick Special at an average speed of better than 88 miles per hour, making only one fuel stop. The $10,000 car, with a straight eight, valve-in-head engine, was capable of 150 miles per hour on a straight away. It was demolished in a crash in the qualifying trials at Indianapolis in 1935.

PUSHMOBILES

The Road Races fascinated Elgin boys who began building their own motorless cars and gave them the names of the big racers they had seen on the west side track—Benz, National, Mercer, Black Crow, Simplex, Knox, Lozier, and Marmon. Bodies came from dismantled wagons, fruit crates, and scrap wood. The steering mechanism consisted of ropes attached to a broomstick and spool, and the steering wheel was a coffee mill casting obtained from the Woodruff & Edwards foundry.

The first racing events were staged in the late summer and fall of 1910. The coasters were either pushed by another boy or, gravity-powered, rolled down one of the many hills of the river city. The driver had the best of it because the "mechanic" had to push all the way up a rise and then jump on the back of the car as it went down a slope. Some of the races were organized with entry fees, adult starters, elimination heats, and prizes for the winners. If wheels spun off, or the steering failed, or the cars collided, the mishaps added to the fun.

By 1915 improvements, such as roller-bearing wheels, had arrived. That was the year pushmobiles on the Division Street hill between Channing and Gifford streets nearly outpaced the police department's new Ford. And it was in 1915 that an inventive 13-year old built a car powered by a gasoline engine connected directly to the rear axle by a belt.

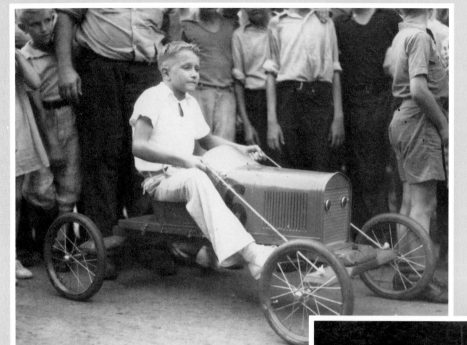

After the one-time revival of the Road Races in 1933, a new generation of Elgin boys was building cars. They caught the attention of Frank (Mike) Danilek and Ed Schuld who had raced in the earlier craze beginning in 1910. With the cooperation of city officials, they organized a race over a four-street course. Each racing team included a driver and pushers who employed a variety of propulsion methods. The event attracted about 3,000 spectators who witnessed spills at the corners and breakdowns from buckled wheels and lost tires. In this 1934 photo a young driver sits in his racer.

The second big race, in 1935, switched from push-mobiles to coasters shooting down a hill. The races became an annual event. Girls were allowed to participate. Some of the vehicles topped 300 pounds and, starting from a ramp, attained rolling speeds of more than twenty miles per hour. The races continued each year through 1942 and then were revived in 1950 and 1951.

It wasn't until 1952 that the first local races were sanctioned by the All American Soapbox Derby based in Akron, Ohio, and subsidized by the Chevrolet Division of General Motors. These races, limited to boys between the ages of eleven and fifteen were held each year through 1959.

PALM SUNDAY TORNADO

13

The city's worst natural disaster, the Palm Sunday tornado of March 28, 1920, claimed seven lives, injured scores, turned a large portion of the business district into rubble and broken glass, and severely damaged more than eighty homes. A violent hail storm and high winds preceded the blast. Then, about 12:23 p.m., there came sudden darkness, a deafening roar, and the tornado cut a swath about two blocks wide through the southwest residential area. It jumped the river near the Milwaukee Road (now Metra) station, wrecked havoc downtown, and blew northeastward up Dundee Avenue.

Automobiles were blown around as if they were toys, and dozens were completely turned over. Hundreds of trees were uprooted, striking houses and shattering windows. Downed telephone poles and wires contributed to the tangled maze on sidewalks and streets. Light and power were cut off, and streetcar service was suspended. Communication with the outside world was cut off for about three hours.

In the aftermath people dug through the debris seeking missing relatives. Mayor Arwin E. Price called up the local militia company to prevent looting and by 5:00 p.m. the downtown area was roped off. The clean up and repair work, which took months to complete, began almost immediately, although it was years before the scars of the catastrophe were completely erased.

Tales of freak occurrences have been passed from survivors to their children and grandchildren. A kitchen knife, blown two hundred yards from a residence, was driven four inches into a tree. An automobile turned completely over and landed on its wheels. Another car was stripped of its top, body and trappings, leaving only the bare chassis standing.

One householder, taking a bath, gripped the sides of the tub and watched his roof blow away. Another was reading a newspaper in his backyard privy. When the storm subsided, he was still seated but the outhouse was a block away.

The Bethlehem Lutheran Church steeple was snapped off at the base, did a somersault while falling, and was deposited on the ground intact. A downtown pedestrian was lifted off his feet, twirled around in the air, pitched through a plate glass window, and emerged with only a few small cuts. A family was sitting in the parlor of their home when the storm lifted the house off the foundation and carried it down the block, leaving the family sitting uninjured in the open air.

When the tornado crossed the river it slammed into the Grand Theater, the George M. Peck department store, and the S. S. Kresge store. Two vaudeville performers applying their make-up, were killed when the walls of the theater crumbled. The pictures above shows the damage to the rear of these buildings, and the other two show what was left of the facades on South Grove Avenue.

The Rev. J. W. Welsh of the First Congregational Church had closed his morning sermon with the reminder, "Today we are here, tomorrow we may be gone," about ten minutes before the storm struck.

"I heard a roar, and on looking up saw the skylight falling through on us and in the main room," he recalled. "I saw the floor sinking into the basement. My first thoughts were for the children who had been attending Sunday school in the basement. I could hear their cries as the floor started to sink. Then the big tower fell in on us, bringing the big roof and gallery with it on the spot where I had been standing a few minutes before."

Two women and a twelve year old girl were killed at the First Congregational Church. At right is the damaged exterior; below, the interior debris. There was one fatality at the First Baptist Church.

The roof of the shoe factory, the only industrial plant to be hit, was lifted off, and the second story lay in a heap on the first floor ceiling. The sprinkler system let go with the impact and flooded machinery and goods in process of work. Hundreds of shoes were swept skyward; some of them were seen floating down the river more than half a mile away. The factory was hit by another tornado in 1933 when the top floor on the west side was blown down.

"I saw cars moving up the street, and there wasn anyone in them" recalled a pedestrian who was hu dled under the awning of a Chicago Street store. "Th tornado went up the street to the First Congregation Church...And then it came back down Chicago, ar the cars came back down with nobody in them. A you could hear was the sound of breaking windows."

One of Elgin's most destructive fires broke out in the wooden Hubbard Block on the northeast corner of Fountain Square on March 23, 1874. The flames, fanned by a strong wind, spread in an easterly direction along Chicago Street, ignited three additional buildings, and jumped across the street to devour Town's Block on the Square's southeast corner. Its walls crashed in with a roar and a brilliant shower of soaring embers. "The streets were filled with men and women, the gale blowing briskly, and the noise of crackling timbers and flying bricks sounded like a fire of howitzers," reported the *Gazette*. "The entire city seemed a sheet of flame, rioting and warring at its own good will."

The heat from the burning buildings was so intense that it cracked glass storefronts on the west side of Grove and blistered the structures on the west side of Douglas. Nineteen business houses suffered heavy losses. The burned out merchants placed signs in front of their former stores. The message of John Newman, who lost his entire inventory in the Hubbard Block, read: "It was too hot to stay."

The *Gazette* described the desolate aftermath: "The ruins smoulder and the fires grow pale and dim, yet they mark a mighty ravage in this little city, and show the fearful power of the fire demon, whose mastery man never yet has achieved."

Some happenings were so unusual or startling they became reference points. "It was before the big fire," or "not long after the great flood." Shared experiences were talked about long afterward. "Where were you when...." and "Do you recall....?"

These "mystic chords of memory" —the phrase is Lincoln's— served to unite otherwise disparate residents of an urban community.

ridges are a necessity in a river city, and their location, cost and conruction have been frequent subjects of controversy. The rambling old ooden bridge across Chicago Street was in poor condition when it was placed in 1867 by a patented Truesdell iron bridge. The roadway was feet wide and planked with solid oak. On the outside of the pedestri walks was an elegant wrought iron railing.

e Truesdell may have been sthetically pleasing but it cked strength. In ecember 1868 more than nety head of cattle, with a mbined weight of about 50-) tons, were being driven ross the bridge when it colpsed. No one was hurt, but tchers had to be sumoned to assist in killing or ving the injured cows.

n the Fourth of July 1869 a owd jammed the railing of e reconstructed bridge to atch a tub race. The east d gave way, throwing spectors into the water. There as one fatality, a woolen ill worker, and many were uised or cut. A Truesdell idge in Dixon, Illinois, llapsed in 1873, killing rty-six persons.

Blizzards in February, March and
April 1881 blocked rail lines and left
snow piled several feet deep in some
places. Ice was frozen to a thickness
of several feet in the river.

When warm spring rains came, the snow melted rapidly and swelled the creeks tributary to the Fox. The ice broke up in huge chunks. A great flood swept down the valley, carrying along farm outbuildings and other debris. The climax came on April 19th when the dam was forced (left) and the river spread out like a fan over both banks. A barn, twisting in the roaring white mass, struck the crumbling supports at the west end of the bridge. Two sections dropped into the water and the rest followed.

Since only the National street bridge was available for pedestrians and teams, the City Council authorized a ferry boat at Chicago Street. The crudely built craft was overcrowded on the morning of April 28th when several school children were crossing, and it capsized in midstream where the current was the swiftest. Boats were quickly launched from both banks as the passengers were borne downstream, their cries piercing the air. Of the twenty-three on board, seven were lost, four of them children.

$300.00 REWARD.

The City of Elgin will pay a reward of $50.00 for the recovery of each body identified as being that of a victim of the late ferry boat disaster. The names and descriptions of the lost, as far as ascertained, are as follows:

THOMAS MURPHY, - aged 35.
GUY CARLISLE, - " 16.
LEO TAYLOR, - - " 16.
JOHN CORBIN, - - " 37.
ELMER FOSTER, - - " 15.
Miss FRANCES A. CREIGHTON, 12.

By order of the City Council.

F. S. BOSWORTH,

Elgin, April 29, 1881.   Mayor.

J. A. Carlisle offers an additional reward of $100 for the recovery of the body of his son. Hair light: slender: shirt marked G. S. C.

The water department's standpipe at Cooper Avenue and Spring Street was formed of riveted and welded steel plates. It was thirty feet in diameter and ninety-five feet in height on a masonry base of twenty feet. At 7:35 a.m. on March 14, 1900, it collapsed in a rush of water, falling ice chunks, and crumpling metal. No one was injured, and property damage to nearby homes was minimal, but people remembered. When an elevated water tank for the west side was proposed in 1913, homeowners objected, and it had to be erected in an undeveloped area along Shuler Avenue the following year. The base of the old standpipe was dynamited in 1914, and the city offered for sale the two lots on which it stood.

The Illinois National Guard
encamped at Wing Park for
two weeks of training in July
1909. About 3,000 infantry,
cavalry and artillery soldiers
drilled and skirmished amid
clouds of dust. They brought
six freight cars of equipment,
including 60,000 rounds of
blank ammunition, and Elgin
merchants supplied the food.
Hotels were jammed, and
stores did a brisk trade.

Street carnivals were held in downtown Elgin in 1901 and 1902. Conderman's Ferris Wheel was a popular attraction at DuPage Street and Grove Avenue. Band members are pictured enjoying a ride. In the background is the Big Boston Clothing Store, formerly the Nolting House. It was replaced by a J. C. Penney store in 1937. The Roman Coliseum was located at the intersection of River Street (North Grove Avenue) and Milwaukee Street (East Highland Avenue).

And of course each year at least one circus came to town and called attention to its attractions by a parade of animals and ornamentally-carved cages "in wealth of display and beauty of coloring." The ever-present small boys are shown here inspecting a steam calliope.

Teddy Roosevelt was immensely popular in Elgin, receiving 85.9% of the major party vote in Elgin Township in the Presidential election of 1904. When he arrived for a brief greeting in 1910, the surging crowd's enthusiasm turned to wild confusion, and he was only able to say four sentences before his train pulled away.

ohn F. Kennedy, ampaigning for the 'residency, spoke to sea of people from platform at uPage Street and outh Grove Avenue n October 25, 1960. e brought no bodyuard. A St. Edward ligh School girl had o be pulled from the ood of his car. This as the first time a najor party candiate for the White Iouse had appeared n Elgin since Vendell L. Willkie vaved from the back f a special train in 940.

189

Elgin's National Guard unit, Co. E, left on September 13, 1917 for Camp Logan, Texas, where it became part of the 129th Infantry, 33rd Division. Hundreds lined the streets and cheered the men, carrying full equipment as they paraded through the streets on their way to the west side North Western station.

Less than twenty-five years later, on March 19, 1941, another local National Guard unit, Co. I, departed from the same west side North Western station for a year of federal national defense training at Camp Forrest, Tennessee. Most of its members would not return home until the end of World War II.

ELGIN'S GREATEST EVENT.

Elgin Pageant of Progress

Aug. 10 to 15

Phone 1550

The big attraction at the Pageant of Progress in 1925 was the city's first bathing beauty contest. Each of the thirty-six contestants was given an Annette Kellerman two-in-one bathing suit. The winner, Lucille Burns, was Elgin's entry in the Miss America contest at Atlantic City. The event was denounced as "demoralizing" and "debasing" by the Ministerial Association. The sponsors replied by asking, "Is the objective of Elgin's citizenry to have a live or dead city? Let us not be prudes but rather broad-minded and progressive."

A huge, 27-passenger Curtis Condor made hourly flights from Burnidge Field along McLean Boulevard in the summer of 1939. The plane had a wing span of 96 feet. More than 3,000 passengers were carried during the aircraft's stay in Elgin.

A *Courier-News* photographer went aloft in the Condor and obtained this birds-eye view of the business district. The Chicago Street bridge is being rebuilt, and a temporary pedestrian bridge can be seen to the right (south). The Highland Avenue bridge was not completed until 1941.

A two-man Japanese submarine was displayed on the Highland Avenue bridge on August 24, 1943. It was captured at Pearl Harbor on December 8, 1941. Admission to the exhibit was gained by the purchase of war bonds or stamps. The windmill at the upper right corner of the picture marks the site of the Elgin Windmill plant.

The largest military
parade ever to be held
in Elgin swung down
South Grove Avenue
on Flag Day, 1943.

193

SONG OF HIAWATHA

"Should you ask me whence these stories, whence these legends and traditions, I should answer, I should tell you—from the land of the Ojibways, from the land of the Dakotas."

For more than half a century, 1927-1979, these words opened the Song of Hiawatha Pageant performed in an outdoor amphitheater at Camp Big Timber. The poem by Longfellow was unabashedly romantic, but the costumes and dancing were authentic. Participants, except for women, girls and children, were Boy Scouts. From a dozen performers around a campfire, the cast and crew expanded to more than 150, all of whom donated their time. The pageant became a family as well as community tradition. The 1974 cast, for example, included 27 offspring of former dancers, and a number of third-generation members.

Carl H. Parlasca ("Injun Par"), left, and his longtime assistant, Evert S. Stoutenburg ("Yellow Thunder").

Director and narrator of the Song of Hiawatha Pageant, Carl H. Parlasca, was a local Boy Scout executive, 1922-1948, who introduced his vast knowledge of Indian and Western lore he acquired on his trips to reservations. Over the years he touched the lives for good of thousands of young people and had become Elgin's Nawadaha, who "sang of Hiawatha...how he lived and toiled, and suffered, that the tribes of men might prosper."

Year after year Elgin audiences were thrilled by the presentation of the myth in an idyllic setting. The program began with the sacred pipe ceremony and traced the growth of Hiawatha from childhood to manhood; his marriage to Minnehaha; her death; the coming of the white man; and Hiawatha's departure for the Land of the Hereafter.

The Big Timber Booster Club, formed in 1934, was a major supporter of the Pageant. Funds were raised by various sales and, beginning in 1944, by wastepaper drives.

Mrs. Par, E. Maude Parlasca, was the first "Old Nokomis" and played the role for 28 years. She was identified in the programs only by her Indian name, *Wa-wo-ki-ye-win*, given to her when she was adopted into the Brule Sioux in 1935.

The Big Timber Dancers participated in many fairs, festivals and parades, such as this one at West Dundee. They appeared at the Scout National Jamboree in 1937 at Washington, D. C. and at the Chicagoland Music Festival in Soldier Field in 1941. With the girl dancers, the *Kwo-Ne-Shes*, they were in the Orange Bowl parade in 1963.

am going, O Nokomis,
n a long and distant journey,
p the portals of the Sunset...

nd the people from the margin
atched him floating, rising, sinking,
ll the birch canoe seem lifted
igh into that sea of splendor...

nd they said, 'Farewell forever!"
id, "Farewell, O Hiawatha!'"

EPILOGUE

After viewing pictures of people, buildings and landscapes that no longer exist, the reader may be reminded of an oft-quoted epitaph:

"As you are now so once was I
As I am now so you must be"

This may be a sobering thought, but change is a constant in American life. The earth, said Thomas Jefferson, belongs always to the living generation. And yet the past is not dead; it is imbedded in our present circumstances, just as what we do today determines our future. It is our responsibility to preserve what is best from Elgin's yesterdays, improve what we can, and transmit this heritage to those who come after us.

BIBLIOGRAPHY

A comprehensive bibliography of Elgin history can be found in
Elgin: An American History by E. C. Alft, 1948, pages 337 to 341.

INDEX

NBD BANK ELGIN
Board of Directors

Carl E. Lundstrom
Chief Executive Officer
Lundstrom Insurance Agency, Inc.
Chairman of the Board,
NBD Bank Elgin

Charles H. Burnidge
President,
Burnidge, Cassell
& Associates

Robert H. Carlile
President &
Chief Executive Officer,
NBD Bank Elgin, N.A.

John A Graham
President,
Sherman Hospital

Charles L. Hines
Officer of Privately-held
Companies in
Retail Clothing Industry

William A. Hoffer
Vice President
Hoffer Plastics

Lane B. Hoffman
President & CEO,
Barco

Roger B. Parsons
President,
Elgin Sweeper Company

John A. Popple
Chairman of the Board & CEO,
Leeward's Craft Bazaar

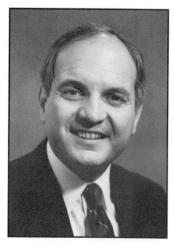

Harry J. Seigle
President, Siegle's Home
& Building Centers

Charles F. Stevenson
Chairman of the Board,
Rinn Corporation

Gregg Ziegler
Chairman of the Board,
Lyle A. Ziegler Hardware Co

200